DANDELION

Once a foster child, always a foster child.

America DeFleur

ISBN: 978-1-945526-53-4

Library of Congress Control Number: 2018913386

Photograph & Cover Design by: America DeFleur
Email: americadefleur@gmail.com
Website: www.americadefleur.com

Edited by: Brenna Kingsbury
Special contributions and additional edits provided by beta readers: David, Kathleen, Renee, Alexis, and Laura

Printed in the United States of America

I Street Press, 828 I Street Sacramento, CA 95814

Kaycee, I'll think of you often, I promise. I'll wonder what you'll look like as you get older, and I'll hope that you enjoy life and experience things that I never had the chance to as a child. I hope one day I'll see you again. You will always be in my heart, little girl.

Lilah, you're my reason for everything. When there was no one else, it was the sound of your voice that kept me going. All my love to my husband, my editor Brenna and everyone who helped me through this process, I couldn't have done it without any of you

To my siblings, I hate to love you and love to hate you. When we were separated, I didn't know what to do except for push forward knowing that one day I'd see you again. To my sister, thank you for always being there for me. To my brothers, I wish we were closer as adults, its lonely.

To the Vadillo, Skinner, Grendahl and Hernandez families, I couldn't have done it without any of you. Thank you for picking up the pieces and taking care of us when we needed it the most.

With Love,

America DeFleur

Table of Contents

Introduction	7
Prologue	9
Into the Dawn	13
Airplanes in the Sky	21
Through Clouds of Smoke	27
Soul Sisters	35
Freedom from this Place	47
Wild as the Wind Blows	53
Cool Watermelon Sunday's	63
Is There Anyone There?	67
Safety is Overrated	75
Eres un Gringa	79
On the Bathroom Floor	85
Is it Over?	91
The Foster Monster	103
A New Life	109
Goodbye Again	115
Strangers Everywhere	121
Growing Up	125
To the Moon and Back	129
In the Middle of the Ocean	135
A New Perspective	143
Epilogue	145
Author's Note	153

INTRODUCTION

It's been exactly ten years since I aged out of a broken system that left me bitter, angry, confused, and lost in a world filled with traumatic experiences and memories that I couldn't escape. Like most youth that have experience with foster care, social services, or adoption, all we ever long for is someone we can look up to, someone who will love us unconditionally and show us that we are worthy of being loved, regardless of what we've been through or what emotional trauma we are experiencing. All we ever yearn for is a place to call home, whether that be the neglectful environment that we were ripped out of, or that perfect home that we've never experienced but always dreamt of.

All I ever longed for was someone to care, someone who could see past all of the angry outbursts or meltdowns that made no sense. Growing up, I wanted someone to save me from the life I endured, to sweep me away, saving me from everything that ailed my broken heart.

I spent the majority of my youth riddled with jealously and an unrelenting anger that never seemed to subside. I wanted things that were essentially built-in for other children, things like: stable, loving parents; food that kept my belly warm; clothes, shoes, jackets and toys; a safe bed to sleep in; someone who listened to me.

I remember picking as many "wish flowers" as I could, thinking that, if magic did exist, and I made a wish hard enough, it would come true. Instead I bounced around from one terrible situation to the next before being shoved out onto the streets at eighteen. I never had that solid foundation to build from or a family to teach me the things that so many others took for granted. That natural bond that most children experience with their parents was stolen from me, taken away by the very people who were supposed to love me most. My mother's bad decisions, drugs, and alcohol had replaced the very essence of the child that stood before her. I was irrelevant. She had been too wrapped up in her own little world to have even the slightest idea that I needed her. My father, when he finally came looking for me, he left me feeling just as broken and used.

Most foster kids, by the time they have reached a certain age, will have built an emotional brick wall that disconnects them from the rest of the world. For a long time, I didn't realize it's what kept me from developing healthy, positive relationships. It's something that took years to establish, and it wasn't something I was able to fix overnight. I thought leaving the system behind and never looking back was the best decision I could make, erasing my past like it had never happened or mattered because at eighteen, "I was an adult and I could make my own decisions." But truthfully, at eighteen, I was still a young, fragile, inexperienced, and sometimes reckless kid. I had problems, and a lot of them, but it wasn't something that a therapist was going to fix either because honestly, I didn't want to accept help or admit defeat.

This is the story of how I almost gave up but eventually found purpose in the lingering pain from my past.

PROLOGUE

"What the...?!" I half-questioned as I stepped through the door, staring at my husband and his lover in disbelief. I stood frozen as they both jumped up in surprise.

"Fuck," she whispered. Her hair was a thin, stringy mess, tossed into a loose bun atop her head. As she fixed her gaze on me, I noticed the dark remnants of makeup shadowing her cheeks and lining the lower sockets of her eyes. "FUCK fuck fuck," she said again.

The dark-haired beauty quickly rolled onto the floor and scurried into the bathroom, locking the door behind her. Jordan tossed the blankets away and jumped off the couch, running toward me with his long lanky legs. I could tell there was still a bit of sleep in his eyes from the way that he rubbed them. I didn't hear a word he said. His lips were moving, but there was no sound. My hands were numb as I unintentionally dug my sharp nails into my palms, releasing a soft, warm liquid that dripped down between my fingers. My voice rose up from the tips of my toes and crawled through my mouth with a fierceness.

"What the fuck is this?! Are you fucking kidding me right now? Are you fucking kidding me?!" I yelled at him. Throwing my purse onto the ground, I grabbed Jordan's shoulders, attempting to shake him, but my arms were weak. My vision blurred through the bits of black mascara that ran down my cheeks. My hands balled back into fists as I fell into him, my eyes darting to the bathroom. I began calling her name. I knew who she was. "You fucking bitch, Becca! GET. OUT. HERE."

"Calm down," she called from behind the door.

"Calm down?! Calm the fuck down?! Are you kidding me?!"

It took a moment before she emerged from the bathroom with her hands in the air. I had never been in a real fight before, but every cell in my body wanted to rip her to shreds, and I was sure there would be nothing left of her once I was finished. As I charged toward her, Jordan slid into place, blocking my path. He held up his hands and said, "It's not about her. It has nothing to do with her. It's me. You want to hit someone? Hit *me.*"

He's right, this is his fault. Everything is his fault.

"Come on! Do it!" He screamed, slamming his fists onto his chest. " I deserve it, so do it!"

And I did. With every ounce of my being, I threw my body into him, scratching, pounding, and slapping as much of him as I could. My bloodied fingers dug into his soft pale flesh for what seemed like an eternity, until my hands found their way to his face. With an open palm, I slapped him until I felt his cheeks burn beneath my fingers. For a while he stood there and let me tear away at him. Then he joined in. He began smacking himself and screaming inaudible words at me. I could hear Becca shouting for help in the background, and suddenly reality set in. Our daughter was asleep in the next room. *I can't let her see this. Stop, America. Stop. Stop. STOP!* But I couldn't tear myself away from him. I wanted to hurt him, wanted him to feel all of the pain I couldn't contain.

As the little concrete steps outside the small apartment rattled with footsteps, I realized people would be coming in any second. An intensely painful sensation began in the pit of my stomach, slowly rising toward my chest and pulling at my lungs, making it hard to breathe. *I need to get out.* Ashamed at what my hands had done, I grabbed my bag from the floor and darted toward the door.

As I pushed past Jordan's neighbors and family, I made my way through the busy downtown streets and toward my parked car a few blocks away. I knew that we were never going to come back from this. *My marriage is over.* Grasping for the car door handle, I flung it open and angrily slammed my body into place in the driver's seat. Shoving the keys into the ignition, I sped off into the early morning mist.

CHAPTER ONE

Into the Dawn

I didn't pack for a trip into the city, but I knew that I needed a change of pace. Things had been out of control lately, and I needed to clear my head, so I got in the car and just drove. At first, I had no idea where I was going or even how long I would be gone, but I had to get away from everything that was familiar, everything that reminded me of Jordan.

Without any real direction, minutes turned into hours as I navigated my way down the road, crying and slamming my fists onto the dashboard while hundreds of fragmented memories raced through my mind. Driven by emotion, I thought about my daughter, my niece, my husband Jordan, my shitty abusive parents, the foster care system, social workers, counselors, siblings, and everyone else I've ever encountered. These memories and thoughts painted such a vivid image of pain and neglect that I could hardly see straight. Speeding down the freeway, I thought about everything that I had endured over the past twenty-four years and decided that enough was enough! Contemplating suicide, I continued to drive into the unknown, laughing maniacally through my tears. Somehow, homeless and alone at 18 was nothing compared to the situation I faced now. *I'm a twenty-four-year-old-soon-to-be-divorced-homeless-former-foster-youth-with-a-kid. I'm the fucking epitome of statistics!*

I didn't want to admit it to myself, but I wasn't ready to be on my own again because this time around, I had nothing. No friends. No family. Nothing. I wasn't sure that I could survive, not with a small child and nowhere to go. I didn't want to become a statistic. I wanted to be different. I always told myself I would be different, but somehow, I was back to square one and exactly where everyone always told me I would be. My life came tumbling down without warning, and I didn't know what to do except drive without looking back.

I held tight to the steering wheel as memories that I had kept at bay came pouring out as if the floodgates of hell had been kicked wide open. Surrendering to my emotions, I was a screaming, sobbing mess as I ran from my past again. Speeding down the freeway in a silver Saturn, I slowly lost myself along the way.

Though he stood outside, his voice echoed through the empty halls of our small house with rage. It must have been a little past midnight when I awoke to his high-pitched screaming.

"You bitch... I know you took it from me! Open the fucking door!" Scott screamed from the steps of our porch.

Not again. I pulled my feet from beneath the tattered sheets and onto the cold stone floor. I could feel the hair on my arms begin to rise as the brisk air caressed my skin. Dragging my feet toward the bedroom door, I pushed it open with a sigh. There, in the middle of the dark hall, were my two younger siblings cuddled together like newborn calves. They sat trembling, their cheeks damp with tears. As I moved closer and their innocent blue eyes met mine, I saw a sense of relief wash over them.

"Quickly! Quickly! Get in your room!" I urged them, hoping they would listen to my stern warning and stay put as I had told them.

"Play with your toys and *stay here*, it's o-o-o-kay," I said, fighting my stutter as I shoved them into the bedroom. My fingers fumbled for the lock on the door as I closed it behind me, safely concealing them within.

The yelling continued as I slowly made my way in the direction of his voice. Stepping into the living room, I could see the reflection of his shadow through the thinly woven curtains that covered the window, and without a word, I placed my body alongside the weary frame. I put my hand over my mouth in an attempt to avoid the pungent smell of mold that encased the window seal beside me, and spying through a tiny slit in the curtain, I watched quietly.

His features were obscured by the depths of the night, but I knew it was undoubtedly him by the sound of his voice. Scott, my mother's young and violent lover, was pacing outside. He placed his hands on his forehead and began clutching at his hair before nervously sweeping it back. His movements were erratic, making me dizzy as his shadow frantically whirled about.

Nights like these were typical, and they usually ended with bruises or cuts that would later scar. Scott would usually arrive unexpectedly, his face rugged and worn like he had been awake for days, and my mother would either get into a fistfight outside with him or stay locked in the house with us as he kicked and pounded at the door for what seemed like hours. But this night was different.

As my eyes began to adjust to the dark, I noticed a pistol dangling from his left hand. My heart stopped. Terrified, I pulled back from the curtain and began fumbling around, looking for my mother as fear swallowed me whole.

There! On the couch. *Fuck.* My mother lay seemingly lifeless on the sofa. I inched toward, hoping that she hadn't overdosed. As I placed my head upon her chest, I heard a faint heartbeat and sighed in relief. My arms were shaking, and I could feel my temperature rise as I began putting the pieces together. *She must have stolen something from him, again.* This wasn't the first time Scott was angry that his "rock" had come up missing, but I had never seen him wield a gun before. Knives, poles, crowbars... even spatulas or rocks, sure. But never this.

"I'll fucking kill you! I'll fucking shoot you all! Open the fucking door!" he screamed. His voice was shaky and loud.

For the first time in a long time, I was unsure of what to do. What I was sure of was that he was going to come in here and shoot us all. I knew that he meant business. I was twelve years old, and I knew that this could very well be the last night of my life if things went sour. *What do I do?*

After a moment of panic, I pulled my thoughts together and began running around the house gathering things to stack in front of the door. Looking for some type of protection, I grabbed the closest kitchen knife and slid into place right below that smelly window with my back against the wall and my butt on the floor. I knew my frail body wouldn't keep him from bursting through that door, but I held my blade tight and prayed.

If he succeeded in barging his way through, a measly kitchen knife would prove useless, but I had to try something. I wasn't sure if I could actually stab him, but I felt much safer with that blade in my hand. With my eyes closed, seconds felt like hours as I sat there under the window, listening to him scream. Every so often, with the flick of his wrist, the pistol he wielded discharged a few bullets and little pellets of metal flew into the air above his head.

As adrenaline and fear raced through me, I began to plan my attack, but no matter how many times I played through the scenario in my head, it never seemed to end well. With a gun in his hand, I simply wasn't fast enough. *Maybe I'll just grab Lillian and Parker and run through the backyard.* "I could jump that fence…it's practically falling over anyway…right? I whispered to myself.

Then I heard a second voice chattering in the distance, maybe even a third. *Are we surrounded? How many people are out there? Oh my god, the kids!* I slid across the floor and scurried back towards the bedroom to check on them. They let out shrill cries as I pounded on the door, urging them to open up. I could see they had been crying heavier than before, eyes swollen, hands shaking.

"Staay-ay stay put, ev-ev-everything is going to b-b-be fine," I stammered, slamming the door behind me. Thoughts of how this could end left an unsettling knot in my throat, but I had to be brave for them.

I wasn't sure if we would all die that night, but I knew that I would do everything in my power to prevent that from happening. As worry turned into fear and then hatred, my hands began to shake, and an uncontrollable energy rose through my body like static electricity. It felt as though every hair on my body was standing straight up. Trying to remain calm, I pressed my lips together in an attempt to keep my emotions at bay, but it was useless.

"Ahhh! FUCK YOU, Scott!" I shouted with uncontrollable rage. *I'm not going to let him get away with this, NOT tonight.* I quickly tossed my messy hair into a loose ponytail and ran back toward the living room, my mouth spewing a stream of profanities.

"The cops are on their way, you son of a bitch!"

"You lying little cunt!" he raged. "Open the fucking door. Now!"

"Hey, Scott?"

"WHAT?!"

"FUCK.YOU."

I held that little kitchen knife firmly and prepared for the worst. I knew that without a phone or any real way of calling for help it was highly unlikely anyone was going to come to save us. *I bet mother never paid the bill—she does that a lot.* The best I could do was lie, hoping he would believe me and leave.

"She's not here! GO AWAY."

It wasn't unlike my mother to disappear for a few days at a time, so perhaps he would believe me, *just* perhaps. Silence washed through the house, and for a moment I thought it worked. "He's g-g-g-gone," I whispered to myself in the stillness of the night.

Then the silence was interrupted by the sound of breaking glass in the kitchen. My heart began to race, and I knew this was it. *It's time. He's in the house. Get up and fight, America.*

I couldn't feel my legs, but I somehow managed to stand. My body was suddenly lighter than it had ever been, my head was spinning, and I could feel my chest tighten from the pressure of holding my breath. Preparing myself for battle, one foot in front of the other, I ran, I screamed, I charged toward the sound of the breaking glass with that frail metal blade above my head.

My voice carried into the night as I flew into the kitchen screaming, but to my surprise I found myself alone standing before a few large rocks that had been thrown in through the window and lay on the floor beneath the table.

"What the...?"

POP! POP! POP!

The sound of gunfire was louder than before and was followed by 2 full-force kicks to the front door. The knife fell from my fingers, and I hit the ground clasping my ears. The world began to slow down, and I felt dizzy. *Have I been shot? Oh fuck, I'm hit.*

With the sound of gunfire still whistling in the background, I began crawling toward Lillian and Parker's room. I could hear the glass crunch beneath my fist, and I felt each sliver pierce my palm, but I kept moving. Crying, praying...*Dear God, if you're out there, help.*

In a haze, I made my way toward the back of the house as the stacked furniture toppled away from the door behind me. Locking my eyes on their bedroom door, I pushed forward. Rubbing my bloody hands vigorously over my body, I searched for a bullet hole, but there was none. *I'm ok.*

Suddenly reality set in and I started moving faster than before. Leaving mother behind, I locked myself in the room with my siblings, waiting for Scott to come in for us. As kick after kick shook that heavy oak door, it didn't budge.

Lillian and Parker fixed their eyes on me, and we exchanged a speechless nod, almost as if to say, *This is it. It's going to happen.*

I held their little hands in my own, squeezing their frail fingers. I lost track of how long we sat holding each other, and then we heard it. Sirens. *Loud* sirens. Suddenly Scott's voice faded into the background. Opening the door, I peered down the hall in a daze. Flashing lights illuminated our entire house like fireworks dancing on the wall, creating a mosaic of shadows and color. We were safe.

—

CHAPTER TWO

Airplanes in the Sky

Staring out my window at the other drivers passing by, I thought about my old life, and how I had left it behind. I thought that leaving everything in the past would allow me to create a whole new life for myself, define my own future, but it didn't. *It left me broken and fucked up!*

As the vineyards came into view in the distance, dizziness washed over me. I thought about a promise I made to myself a long time ago. I thought about everything I always wanted, and about the tiny beautiful wish flowers I used to pluck from fields of dying yellow grass. I remembered what it felt like to place the small, soft seeds against my lip and blow as hard as I could, sending fragments of dreams into the air above. I wished for a family, for people to love me, for someone to take me away from every unstable home I never felt safe in.

Over the years my list continued to grow, and my dying wish flowers continued to scatter the sky with my dreams. *Why does it still hurt so much?* I could feel the little girl inside me begging to be seen, tearing at my seams, urging me to remember the way it felt to want things people took for granted daily. Clothes, shoes, toothbrushes, makeup, socks, sweaters that were warm and fuzzy and made me feel safe. I wanted everything I never had, but above all, I wanted somewhere to belong.

When I found Jordan, everything seemed to fit into place perfectly. I thought we stood a fighting chance at conquering the world together. *So how did we get here?* I slammed buttons on the dashboard, looking for a song on the radio to drown my thoughts in.

"Ugh, you piece of shit radio!" I screamed at the top of my lungs as the static from empty channels filled the space around me. "I'm never going to love anyone again, EVER!"

It sounded ridiculous out loud, and a piece of me knew it wasn't just about Jordan. I knew to the depth of my bones that this frustration and anger that shrouded my soul had been there for years. Something inside me was missing, and I couldn't quite explain it, but it was like a hole deep within my chest, a lingering void that prevented me from living a normal, stable life. It withered away my very essence. Jordan was just another casualty of the inevitable, proof that everyone will eventually let you down or give up.

I'll never trust anyone again! Fuck the world. The faster I drove, the quicker I was able to repeat the words, and the easier it was to speed into my future knowing I'd never hurt like this again. *I'm going to find a peaceful place to die.* Smashing my foot against the pedal, I sped down the freeway. Tiny planes soared in the distance triggering a childlike happiness I had long forgotten. A time before Scott came into the picture. In that moment, watching the planes sweep through clouds above me, I thought about my brother, and how much I missed him. Memory after memory fell down my tear-stained cheeks.

"We gotta do the airplane, Bradley!" our little voices would announce as we all jumped for joy. My big brother would then take his place on the ground lying flat on his back and position his feet under our bellies. One by one he would lift us high into the air and parallel to his body. First Parker, then Lillian, and lastly me.

Placing his hands on our stomachs for stability, he became the ground from which we soared. I would fly atop his legs for what seemed like hours, disappearing into an innocent bliss with my big brother. As he swayed his feet back and forth, I would spread my arms wide and picture myself high above the clouds, soaring far away from that little dope house on the corner that we called home. Like a high-pitched vacuum, he roared with silly sounds from below, and I laughed with my siblings, giggling together like children should. Nothing else mattered, and for a moment we escaped the world around us.

It wasn't always like that, though. He had his cliché big brother moments when he told us dinosaurs lived in water towers and the clouds never moved, or he would say things like: "That's because you were found in a trash can." "Have you looked at yourself in the mirror? You're brown and adopted." Then he would laugh.

Barely old enough to spell, I had begun to believe him. Did I come from somewhere else? *Mommy doesn't like me anyway.* We were never planned, it's true. I could tell by the way she talked to us. I could feel the lingering resentment in her words. She wanted to hurt us, she wanted to blame Bradley for how much of her youth he had taken from her.

She was barely a kid herself when she gave birth to Bradley. Sixteen years old, and she never had the chance to go to high school or win prom queen. "I was a knockout!" or so she would say, showing us pictures of a younger version of herself in a red bikini. She married a fresh-faced military man and flew all over the world with him, then spent a few years in Japan raising my eldest brother until she realized she didn't love her husband.

It wasn't long before the life she never wanted caught up with her. They divorced when Bradley was just a toddler, and it was all too easy for his father to take Bradley. She hadn't been a fit mother for years, indulging in drugs and frequent drinking— the woman liked her freedom. So, when his father came and took him away, there wasn't much of a fight to keep him. Bradley was taken away from her, and she spent the following years single, drowning in men, liquor, and drugs, and making more babies. Making us. First me, then Lilian, and last but not least, Parker.

I always thought Bradley had it the easiest. He was a few years older than I was and had an outlet to escape. When things weren't going too well, or when mother burst into a drunken fit, Bradley would take a few of her angry punches and leave, but not before he burst a few holes into the wall first. He never laid a hand on her but always managed to end up with bloody knuckles as he sped down the alley on a skateboard or left in the backseat of his father's car. His visits usually ended with an escape.

As we grew older, I envied Bradley because he got to escape her permanently—the military swept him away like a cold stream on a hot summer day. There he learned to be brave, strong, obedient, and smart. He was given a chance to start fresh and make something of himself. He was going to become a new person and lead a life away from all the trash and filth that surrounded us. When he joined the service, it was hard watching him go because then we knew the weekend visits with him would end. He lived with his father most of our lives, but it was refreshing when he would come and visit, he made us feel like kids again, he made us forget. He protected us. Then he left us with her, and for the longest time I didn't understand why my big brother would just leave us behind. I was always angry with him, but as the years went on and I got older, I wished I could escape with him.

There are things I'll never forget, like the time she disappeared for days on a drinking binge with Allie, our neighbor. I was 9 years old and stood in the doorway with nothing but an oversized T-shirt on. *She left us again.* Slamming the door, I ran back to my siblings to see if they were awake or knew where mother had gone. She had vanished without a word, and I knew it could be days before she resurfaced. *Stupid Allie. Stupid mother.*

Swimming through piles of clothes, garbage, and broken toys, I fought my way to the bedroom where I climbed on top of the bed next to Lillian and Parker. *I shouldn't wake them.* As I lay next to them, I wrapped my arms around their little bodies and cuddled up close, holding them. I knew that when they woke up, it would hit them harder than it had me, so I placed my hands in each of theirs and cried myself back to sleep beside them. With their tiny hands resting in my palms, at least I knew we had each other. We always had each other.

We didn't have a mommy, so I played the role. It was up to me to take care of them, and I knew that. If that meant eating Cheerios and peanut butter for the next three days, then that's what I fed them because it was the only thing I knew how to make. It was also the only thing we had in the cupboards. It took all my strength to push that chair across the chipped linoleum. It was so much bigger than my little self, but I moved it nonetheless. In tears, I would place my little foot on the cushion and pull myself up onto the counter, then I would search the cupboard above my head for my box of goodies.

I was so proud of myself for being able to show Lillian and Parker how to dip a dirty spoon in peanut butter and cover it in Cheerios. I tried my best to turn it into a fun game, and most of the time it worked. They loved watching the spoon catch little round o's as they shook the peanut butter coated metal around in the box. Laughing, we would all shove mouthfuls of tasteless filler into our bellies, waiting for her return.

As much fun as we had together, it still lingered in the back of my mind that mother was gone again. Half the time we didn't know where she went, when she was coming back, or if we would even see her again. *Is this the time she leaves us for good?* It was like that most days growing up—we always found ourselves alone. Day by day we lived in fear, and each night we waited, forced to distract ourselves by any means necessary.

"Can you count again? Pahhweaase? Last time, I promise," Lillian begged.

They were so tiny, their little bones nearly bursting through their skin as they would stand there in yellow- stained shirts looking up at me, waiting for an answer.

"Fine, but this is the *last time,* and no hidin' outside!"

"M'kay! You're it!"

"One...two...three..."

I wish I could forget how hungry we were while our mother was gone, how terrified I was, and how for days, I had to console my younger siblings and feed them lies about when mommy would be back.

I knew it was wrong, I knew that other kids weren't swimming through piles of debris that rotted on the floor for weeks, leaking a putrid smell into the air. I knew that other children didn't have to wait at the front door, or lurk outside, wondering if they would see their mother again. She left us again and again, and it wasn't until she started bringing random men home for sex that I stopped waiting for her return and started wishing she would never come back.

CHAPTER THREE

Through Clouds of Smoke

Miles out of the city and past the apple orchards, I pulled my car over near a little dirt patch on the side of the road. With no recollection of how long I had been driving or how I even got there, I threw open the car door and began heaving into the dirt as cars raced past. *I miss Bradley so much. Why did he leave us?*

Overwhelmed with emotion, I wiped my face with the corner of my sleeve, combed my hair back into place with my fingers and rested my chin against the steering wheel. Looking at the sign ahead of me, it read: Dixon 8. Vacaville 19. San Francisco 62.

San Francisco seems like a beautiful city to leave everything behind in. I had always loved that golden bridge and the way that city never sleeps. It was then, on the side of the freeway, that I began to actually plot my demise. *Maybe I'll visit the ocean one last time before plunging to my death off that bridge. It'll be a quick death, and then I'll disappear beneath the waves for good.*

Wallowing in self-pity, thinking about everyone I would be leaving behind and everything I would be giving up, I suddenly became dizzy again. Frantically throwing my door open, I began purging a steady stream of this morning's breakfast until there was nothing left for my body to let go of. The thought of not being here anymore sent waves of cold, sweaty chills down my spine, but somehow, I also found solace in knowing that my pain

---

would cease. I needed a minute to breathe, to feel something other than this unbearable pain.

I pressed my fingers on the little button near the top of the dashboard and listened to the hazard lights as they clicked off and on over and over again. I could feel the car rock slightly with each vehicle that hurtled past. My phone had died a few miles back—*not that anyone will be calling me anyway*—and I didn't keep people close. My friends were few and far between, mostly because I could never bring myself to trust anyone. I was a terrible friend anyway.

I could never seem to stay in contact with people, and after so many years of bouncing around, I lost faith in humanity altogether. I suppose it was a way of protecting myself after so many years of negligence. The ability to shut people out was a "skill" that I had. It was easy to keep people at a distance, especially when I knew that they would inevitably let me down or hurt me. Jordan was the first person I relied on after leaving foster care. *And he is going to be the last person to break my heart.*

Without a map or any real way to tell where I was going, I decided to sit until my thoughts cleared and I could muster up the strength to continue driving into the oblivion. I looked at the green road sign outside my window. I knew the signs would guide me, but I wasn't actually sure I could make it to San Francisco without some type of navigation. After a few deep breaths, I slid my keys into the ignition and eased my car back onto the busy freeway. It had become a bit easier to breathe with an objective in mind and a moment's rest. *Goodbye, world.*

"Bitch, it's my turn."

"No, fuck you, it's my turn."

"Gimme the blunt, George!"

As my siblings and I sat on the moldy bed, holding bits and pieces of broken toys, we thought nothing of the shouting that came from beyond the doorway. It was a typical day for us. People were continually coming in and out of that little beige house on Harris Avenue, Tori's house. Tori, mothers so-called "best friend," though I knew better. *Druggie friend is more like it,* let us live with her momentarily while mother claimed to get better. They constantly enabled each other, getting high on a daily basis.

Some nights, little white lines of powder lay scattered across the table in the living room while they rolled large round blunts of their favorite "Mary-J-Wanna." Other nights, the house was filled with grungy men who wore dirty clothes with too many holes and fringed leather jackets. Some of her "friends" were thin, frizzy-haired kids who only stayed for a minute to swap a handful of cash for a few bags of whatever my mother stashed between her boobs.

Mother was frail, and every strand of her once-beautiful hair was cheaply stained with a variety of blonde shades. Her beauty wasted away with every heroin injection, and I could sense her love for us lessen with every line of cocaine she snuffed from rolled photographs of us, photographs that used to hang on the walls of our house. Slowly, over time, she faded. Heavy bags hung below her brown eyes, and her high cheekbones were shrunken, which seemed to exaggerate her dilated pupils even more.

Most times, when she was lonely and starved for another high, random men would come into the house and fill her void. Mother and her friend, Tori would lay paralyzed and half-coherent, fading in and out of consciousness on the sofa, as strangers ran their hands across their inner thighs. The men would grunt with excitement as they stripped themselves of their clothing to mount each woman.

Some days she would make me stand in the doorway, forcing me to watch, urging me to pull a sheet of tobacco paper and roll another cigarette for her. Slipping the thin paper between my lips, I would lick the sheet closed and pass her another "rollie" while she laughed.

"This is how you please a real man, baby," she'd babble, half-awake with a cigarette hanging from between her lips. I can still see their shadowy, grim faces staring back at me. Sometimes they would smile a cold, empty smile that made the hair on my body stand straight up. I would stand there sobbing quietly, waiting for mother to wave me back into the bedroom so I could join my siblings and take them into the attic to hide from the strange men.

Tori's house was riddled with a sickness that never seemed to leave, a sickness of the mind that consumed mother quickly and left us fending for ourselves more often than not. Our safe place was in the attic, away from everyone and everything that roamed in through that unlocked front door. Tori's youngest son was nearly eleven and about a year or so older than me. He learned how to cope with his mother's addictions by converting the attic into a bedroom and hiding away.

In order to get up there you had to jump across a gaping hole on the bathroom floor where the toilet used to be just to reach the ladder. Though our hideaway kept the strangers out, it didn't prevent the rancid smell of burning rubber from seeping through the cracks when everyone downstairs was smoking or cooking their next batch. When the stench was too much to bear and we could no longer breathe from the intoxicating fumes, we would open a small window. Giggling, we would all leave our toys and paper magazines behind and leap outside, sliding down the rain gutter screaming, "You're it!"

"No, *you're* it!"

"Hide and seek!!"

"No, cops and robbers!" Parker would shout as we all ran down the street, running further and further away from that little dope house on the corner. I knew it was wrong, every frail bone in my body knew that *this* was wrong, but I couldn't tell her that, not while she was high. Most conversations with her never ended well when she was intoxicated.

"They are watching me! He is bald! I can't let them see me...GET RID OF THESE HOLES! HIDE, HIDE NOW!" mother called.

She had convinced me that tiny cameras were placed within every visible hole in our house. She made me search the walls and fill every crevice with little wads of wet toilet paper so they couldn't see us. I never knew who "they" were, and I never questioned. My hands would shake as I stuffed wet toilet paper into the smallest cracks on our ceiling. I would swiftly move chairs from place to place as I climbed and filled for what seemed like hours, afraid of what would happen if I didn't help her. She would sit there with a cigarette in her hand, ranting, and every so often she would peer out of the window, looking into the distance at nothing. I could tell she was waiting for something to happen, but nothing ever did.

"Do you see them? Right there in the TV. LOOK!"

"There's nothing there," I sighed with exasperation

"They are staring at us, RIGHT THERE," she proclaimed, pointing to the television.

"Th-th-th-the TV is off," I stuttered.

"Open your fucking eyes, America. Look at those two men right there. They are sitting on the couch next to me, staring at us," she said matter-of-factly.

As we got older, mother got worse. She could usually be found passed out face-first onto the table or roaming the streets in search of soda cans and bottles to recycle for cash. Money to fund her addiction. Eventually, I became so frustrated that when she least expected it, I would grab her little hidden white bags of cocaine and drain her bottles of liquor before she could finish them. Enraged, she would chase me down the hall, ripping at my long thick hair, twirling it around her fist to try and stop me.

"AMERICAAAAA, you FUCKING STOP RIGHT NOW!" she would scream.

"No! Let me go! Screw you!" my tiny voice would rattle off. I would swing my small fists at her as she released the firm grip she had on my hair. Running down the hallway, I would dart into the bathroom and shove the door closed behind me, fumbling to flush her drugs down the toilet. She would always burst through the door to catch me, but not before half of her little bag went swirling into the drain below. Then, I would make my escape as she scrambled to collect whatever powdered happiness she could find scattered across the bathroom floor. *Fuck you mother. Take that!*

When I wasn't angry with her, I continuously searched for affection that she never seemed to give. When I would try to cuddle her in the middle of the night, she would get angry. "What the fuck are you doing? Get off me, you little shit!" she would shout, shoving me to the floor. "Go back to your room!"

When she would get angry, she would search for anything nearby to throw at us. It turned into a game after a while. We, the "hellions," would try to dodge whatever objects came hurling at us. Anything she could fit in her hand fast enough to throw, she did. Shoes, pictures frames, plates, lamps, leather belts, or books, they all came flying at us whenever our voices annoyed her, or whenever we wouldn't "shut the fuck up."

The bruises usually faded quickly, unless we weren't fast enough to dodge the belt and she really hurt us. To this day, half of Bradley's tooth is still missing from that time she slapped him in the face with a metal-rimmed belt buckle. One year he went "skateboarding" and fractured his arm, but we all knew better. Half the time I don't think mother really knew what she was doing. The world she lived in wasn't the one that existed around her. She wanted to be free of the children that weighed her down.

"Free of you little shits!" "You little shits!" "Oh, you little bitch!" "Come here ya fucker!" We had so many different names after a while. Even if I tried, I couldn't pinpoint the day she stopped loving us, but it hadn't always been like that. When we were very young and still learning how to talk, she read us to sleep and tucked us in at night. Every now and then she would sing us sweet nothings until our eyes fluttered closed.

"Don't let the bedbugs bite. If they do, pick up a shoe and beat them black and blue... doot ...doot da doo," her soft voice whispered. But that was a long time ago, before the drugs swallowed her whole.

CHAPTER FOUR

Soul Sisters

As my car cut through the early frosty wind, I pushed forward, trying to forget the words that I had grown so accustomed to hearing: "No one likes you." "You are going to be alone for the rest of your life." "You're *trash* just like your mother." "When you're pregnant, alone, and on welfare, don't come knocking on my door." I occasionally glanced at myself in the mirror, watching the tears fall down my face. *You deserve this, go kill yourself.*

It was as though watching the pain seep from my eyes made me feel better. I wanted to cry. I wanted to believe everything people had been telling me for years. Because if it were anything other than true, I wouldn't be here right now. I wouldn't be speeding a hundred miles away toward a city to escape. *I wouldn't be alone while my husband lay wrapped in another woman's arms.* As I pressed my foot harder against the pedal and clenched the steering wheel tighter, I pictured them together on our sofa.

I wanted to call someone, say my goodbyes as I sped down the freeway. Just one last conversation. But then I realized that I had no one. The only person I wanted to talk to was Jordan. *Does she love him? Could they ever love each other like we used to?*

Before everything broke, before other people came into the picture, before we lost it all, I had just turned 18 and aged out of the system. Forced out and onto the cold hard streets of the city, I roamed around for months after I turned eighteen. At first, it was difficult, knowing that I was alone in a sea full of people that could all care less about a little ol' street rat like myself. It took a while before I became comfortable with the idea of sleeping with a knife to stay safe. I could never stay in one place too long, and always made sure that no matter what I did, I put distance between myself and other people because no one could be trusted. I used to love roaming, seeing new things, exploring different parts of the city I hadn't been to before. The trees in the capital park were always full of ripe, round oranges that I would steal and tuck away in my pack before being chased out by security.

When Jordan and I started dating, we spent every possible waking minute together. Once he found out I had been living on the streets, he insisted that I move in with his family. Without telling his parents, he dropped me on their doorstep like a lost puppy. They were shocked and already overwhelmed in a small apartment with their large family, but they couldn't turn me away. He wouldn't let them.

I had a difficult time adjusting to my new life with him, trusting him, and his family. I knew they wouldn't hurt me, but my relationship with them was difficult to sustain. No matter how much I tried to fit in, they reminded me that I was just another outsider. As messed up as they were, I wanted to be a part of their family so badly. They possessed an eerie sense of something "familiar" that drew me to them like a magnet. I wanted to belong.

His father's drunken outbursts didn't scare me, the weed and chain smoking cigarettes didn't keep me away. His drugged-up sister and her aggressive boyfriend was nothing new to me. I didn't worry because he kept me safe and made me feel loved. But after time, things were becoming more difficult than ever to uphold. Somewhere between the drama that unfolded daily and the demons that consumed them all, it became too much for me. They always made it seem like I was never good enough.

It was a losing battle from the beginning and I knew it. But I loved him in my own twisted way and refused to give up. As "familiar" as their broken lifestyle was, it was tearing us apart and hurting me.

Eventually we moved out and into an abandoned apartment by ourselves. For months, we stole electricity from neighbors with a thick orange cord and cooked TV dinners in a toaster oven. We showered in cold water and stole toilet paper form the local target down the street. We worked meaningless jobs, ate pizza until we fell asleep and rode bicycles along the outskirts of the city every day looking for adventures. After about a year, I eventually settled down as a cashier to earn a stable income while watching my belly grow. I was creating a little human of my own. *Finally, someone that was going to love me no matter what, just like he did.*

With the passing months, we stayed away from his family even though they seemed to accept me more as the pregnancy progressed. Every now and then we took help from them when they weren't drunk and didn't hate me. But soon after our daughter was born, we moved far away and into a real working apartment with electricity. The little person growing inside me motivated us to do something better with our future. Lilah, my little human. From the moment her eyes met mine, I knew that we were going to give her everything I never had.

His love saved me, and her loved saved us. But after a while, Jordan and I began falling apart. It was a slow progression over years, a multitude of tiny things that clouded our love for one another. It was years of struggling together and a burrowing resentment we held onto while trying to make ends meet each day. It was the pressure of my past while struggling to create a

---

37

future without guidance. It was the loss of our niece Kaycee whom we fostered and took from his addict sister when Lilah was three years old. We were going to adopt Kaycee one day, and then it all became too much.

When we finally made it, the weight of everything else came crashing down. We were exhausted. We became excellent roommates and forgot how to love each other and, in the process, stopped caring. We were too busy paying the rent, feeding the kids, and going to work. We were so consumed with bettering our lives that when we weren't bickering about everything under the sun, we were escaping reality in other ways. Indulging in childlike video games to escape the life we built with one another.

We were better roommates than lovers, and then that's exactly what we stayed. Roommates until the day he drove away in a truck packed with tiny boxes, and the furniture my ILP worker gave us the day we bought our first apartment together.

I couldn't believe that after everything we had been through this was where we ended up. I thought I had found the person I was going to spend the rest of my life with. I was sure of it, in fact. *How naive and stupid was I to think anyone would stick around? This is just another messed up version of losing yet another person I love,* I thought as I rolled down the car window to breathe in the ocean fog.

As I roared through the rolling hills a few miles before entering the city, I thought about my time with Jordan and how we used to love each other with a fierceness. Trying my best to push the memory of what we used to have out of my head, I continued on. *There's no going back now.*

I knew that what I was going to do was wrong, I knew it from the depth of my soul, but I didn't care because I also knew the only person that would miss me would be my daughter. *And she's too young to miss me, really.* I kept telling myself that, we don't really start forming memories until we were at least seven. *She'd hardly need me.* I knew her father would take care of her, and I believed that she was better off without me. *Maybe I'm the reason for all this? Maybe it's just me. I'm weak and tortured by my past. I'm too fucked up to give her everything she deserves. I can't do it.*

Repeating a multitude of different excuses to myself, I attempted to justify what I was about to do. It didn't feel like suicide, it felt like letting go of everything that held me down. *I should have offed myself a long time ago. I just wish I had one last person to talk to right now. Piper I miss you.*

"Put these on, they're my stepdads," Piper exclaimed as she handed me sweatpants and a grey sweater three sizes too big.

"Are you sure this is going to work?" I asked, grabbing the sweater she handed me.

"Are you kidding me? I do this all the time. Are you hungry or not?

"Yeah, o-o-o-h k let's go."

"Have you ever stolen anything before?"

"No."

I had met Piper in 7th grade. She was the first person to compliment my botched hair dye job. I wanted something to change, some aspect of myself to be just a little bit different, so I swiped a box of mother's Revlon Colorsilk hair dye.

I was going to look like the beautiful blonde on the box, but what was supposed to be a few highlights ended up as orange chunks of chemically burned hair that I couldn't fix. My dark locks just didn't take the bleaching very well.

"I fucking told you not to touch my shit. Guess you learned your lesson now, huh?" mother said. But Piper told me I looked beautiful, "The color really accents your face. I like it!" From that day forward, we were inseparable. I had never had a best friend before.

Piper and I had a lot in common, so it was easy to connect with her. We both thrived in broken environments, both of our mothers were less than normal but we never let that define us. We had a shared passion for music and art. Sketching pictures for hours, we would exchange stories and giggle. Piper had beautiful green eyes that would sometimes change color depending on her mood, and her hair was long and thick, coarse like a stallion but as golden as the sun. When she laughed, she would throw her head back, uncontrollably giggling while her hand covered her mouth, concealing her gapped teeth. We protected each other, both at school and home.

At eleven, Piper had been on her own for quite some time, so she was a bit more street savvy than I was, and she made sure to never let us go hungry. Mother received food stamps every month and would bring us with her to collect booklets full of colorful dollars so that we could buy groceries. But the money never seemed to last long. The booklet was thick and filled with ones, fives, tens and twenties that could be torn out. They were comparable to cash, but we could only buy food with them *If you weren't my mother that is* - the majority of the time she sold them before we could go shopping. We were just walking dollar signs to her. We were beneficial for her lifestyle, so she endured us.

"I can get fifty cents on the dollar for this! Gets your hands off!" she would snap, ripping the colorful toy money away.

Food was scarce, and I could only bring home so many school lunches to feed Lillian and Parker dinner. We were quickly running out of food, which is why I counted on Piper to pull us through this in one piece. She devised a plan to fill our pockets with food because the fridge had been empty for days, and mother refused to do anything about it. "Stop whining and eat something at school" she would say. But weekends became tough when there wasn't a cafeteria lady shoving little squares of cheese pizza and cubed meat onto our lunch plates. Lillian and Parker couldn't understand why mother wouldn't give us anything to eat, so Piper and I took it upon ourselves to feed them. We knew it would be a few days before we had another meal and frankly we couldn't wait that long. So, on Friday before school let out, we ditched second period to run down the street and prepare for the days to come.

"I'm gonna show you how to do this, but don't act suspicious okay?" she whispered as we walked toward the entrance of the grocery store.

"What is that supposed to mean? How am I supposed to act?"

"Just act normal. Fill up the shopping cart, and every now and then just put something in your pants. It's not that hard, Jeez," she said, annoyed.

Walking inside, Piper and I grabbed a squeaky metal cart and began pushing it around the store, casually talking to one another while attempting to pull off the impossible. As we rummaged through the aisles, smiling at people and stuffing our pockets when no one was looking, our pants became heavier and heavier.

"America, get the butter," she whispered,

"I don't have any more room, we have to leave."

As we made our way to the register with our shopping cart, we began placing items on the belt and started up a small conversation with the cashier just to keep things casual. By the time the total was announced, Piper was already rummaging through her wallet, pretending to find something that wasn't there.

"Oh my gosh, my mom has the money in the car. Do you mind If we go out and grab it really quick? she asked the cashier.

"Yeah we'll be right back! Can you h-h-hold this for us p-p-please?" I hated stuttering.

Nodding her head, the fresh-faced girl gave us permission to leave. "But hurry back!" she said.

We strolled through the front door, made our way around the corner of the building, and never looked back. As we made our way through the parking lot, we didn't speak. I kept waiting for Piper to say something, or for someone to grab me by the shoulders and drag me back into the store, but nothing happened. Approaching the house, she placed her hand on my shoulder and smiled. "I told you it would work." I never left Piper's side after that.

Not long after our little shoplifting operation, mother had lost her job, the house, and pretty much everything we owned. For a while, we stayed with our grandmother and uncle who baked biscuits from scratch and showed us how to cook spaghetti. But our stay with them was always short- lived and usually ended with our mother drunk, fighting everything and everyone in her path. They always begged her to leave us behind, but she never did. For the next few months, we bounced around between sleeping on the streets, and sleeping in homeless shelters near the homeless district.

The homeless district was a large community of people that lingered together near the outskirts of downtown, looking for resources and help. "Loaves & Fishes - Friendship Park" they called it, but it was far from friendly and looked nothing like the typical green grassy fields that you would imagine a park to be.

It was a tiny street that was always overcrowded. Most people pushed little carts or pulled along barrels of clothing, carrying backpacks with everything they owned strapped to them. Everyone needed a bed to lay their head on at night, so we all gathered in lines near the entrance to the shelters, waiting for them to open the solid metal door nestled within little tiny brick buildings.

Further down the private street, large warehouse garages lined the paved roads and though I never knew what was inside, I always found myself wondering. *Maybe they are little tiny testing labs where they torture people.*

Next to the shelters and encapsulated within the community, there was a school that we went to occasionally, "Mustard Seed" was a strange collection of cottage like houses located onsite near the shelters where children were stationed to receive somewhat of an education while parents attended a variety of classes to help correct their behaviors, cope with abuse, put them on the right path, or educate them about the effects of anger and abusive relationships. "See, it's just like we are all going to school together" mother would say before running off to another WEAVE counseling session. She was enrolled in every program possible while we were taught general studies. Public school just isn't an option when you're homeless.

The shelters were challenging to get into because there was such a massive amount of people lined up waiting. Men's shelters were typically segregated from women. When it came to family shelters, they usually prioritized availability to mothers and children, but it was never guaranteed. On the days we didn't make the list to sleep at a shelter that night, we waited in another line behind a multitude of people, sitting stagnant in sweat and dirty clothes, hoping that there would be enough space on the charter bus, so we wouldn't have to sleep on the streets again.

We would all sit there for hours and whine under the hot sun as it blistered our faces, waiting for the charter bus to arrive and take us away to a sanctuary for the night. The homeless district just didn't have the capacity to give everyone a warm bed and a shower, so the remaining people were taken in busloads to a makeshift campsite at the local fairgrounds-Cal Expo. Only a few miles away from downtown, the campsite was composed of portable buildings, and inside them were rows upon rows of bunk beds and fold out tables that we used for an early breakfast the next morning before they shipped us back. Every morning at Friendship Park we would wait for a little old woman to roll out a cart with hot coffee, tea, and hot cocoa for everyone. Mother would sip her coffee and slide her tongue across a thin sheet of tobacco paper, sealing it shut. We sipped on hot cocoa and waited for Mustard Seed to open while mother smoked up a storm.

For the next few months, our lives consisted of the same few things, day in and day out. Waiting. Sitting. Crying. Begging. Sleeping. Bus. Breakfast. Cocoa. Mustard Seed. Sleeping. Wash, rinse, and repeat.

As I looked around at all the strangers and all the carts they carried around with them, I'd think to myself how terribly sad everyone looked, how worn and weathered their faces were. Most days it didn't feel real. The fake smiles and spoons full of mush they fed us left a hole where my heart should have been. It felt like a dream, an endless waking nightmare that I couldn't escape. Lost in a haze, I would watch carts filled to the brim with aluminum cans peddle by, all we could do was survive.

This couldn't be right? To everyone else-Lillian, Parker, our mother-it all seemed so natural. I hated it. I felt out of place, I felt cheated out of a good life, and I blamed my mother. *She couldn't keep things together, and we had to suffer.*

I constantly wallowed in self-pity because I knew there was something better out there, a life completely opposite to the one I'd been living. A life where I could wake up one day and pull clothes out of a drawer that smelled of freshly scented flowers. A place where I didn't have to shower in a room full of strangers exchanging handfuls of miniature shampoo bottles that barely fit in my hand. I knew there was a life where I didn't have to worry about who was sleeping next to me in the bunk over. I was surrounded by smelly, loud, shaky people rocking themselves to sleep. At night when I couldn't keep my eyes closed, some of the staff members that took the nightshift would coax me into their office with a ball of yarn, and like a little kitten I would unravel endless streams of colorful string for the little old ladies to crochet with as we chatted. After a few weeks, they began showing me how to stitch together little squares. *This is kind of nice...*

Weeks turned into months as I transitioned in and out of shelters with my family, carrying balls of yarn with me wherever I went to keep my fingers busy. Crocheting was fun and challenging. It helped me focus on something other than the hardships we endured. Soothing a deep rage within, I would crochet until I couldn't hold the hook between my fingers any longer.

Every now and then I would escape to Piper's house and leave my siblings and mother behind at the shelters. Mother never seemed to care much, and hell, it was one less kid to keep an eye on at the District. Every so often I would spend the night sleeping next to Piper in her bed, or on the couch where it was nice and warm. I always felt bad for my siblings at night. I didn't like leaving them stranded in "Friendship Park," but they never seemed to notice. They were so young, and much too busy at Mustard Seed to care To me, the homeless district was just another place I couldn't wait to escape.

CHAPTER FIVE

Freedom from this Place

A s the early morning mist turned into thick fog, I knew I was approaching the city of San Francisco, and a sense of calmness washed over me. As I stuck my hand out of the window, it disappeared. I was shocked at how easily the fog engulfed my hand, covering it in a shroud of what seemed like nothing. I could almost feel each molecule of water in the atmosphere. Blindly driving through the blanket of nothingness, it was difficult to see the road ahead of me. I cracked the car door open slightly as I released my foot on the pedal, coming to a slow. With the door open just enough to see the ground a few inches below, I continued on, hoping white lines would be enough to guide me through the condensed haze.

Rolling down all of my windows, the temperature in my car dropped quickly as the dense air filled the inside of my vehicle and cool thick air caressed my wet cheeks. While thick wisps of wind blew against my face, I became lost in that density. I felt the weight of a fog that I've carried around me for years unravel itself slowly. My childhood was consuming me, and I was drowning.

—

"Pack your shit, we're leaving" mother said stumbling past us. It wasn't long before mother was kicked out of every program known to man and banished from the system after making our way through the shelters, and through multiple transitional facilities. She exhausted all of her resources because she couldn't put the bottle down in a "Clean and Sober Living Environment." I knew I needed to leave, for my own sanity, but not until Lillian and Parker were stable. It took a while of bouncing around from house to house before mother somehow managed to find a home she could afford with government assistance.

It was a little white house with a small picket fence on Glenn Avenue that had a glorious willow tree covering the front porch. The same porch that Scott later fired rounds of bullets into. That was the last night I spent in that house before finally deciding to leave them behind and venture into the world on my own. As much as I loved Lillian and Parker, I couldn't be there for them anymore. I was tired of being *their* mother. I wanted to hurt less and live more. I was so sick of the unknown and the worrying.

As much as I didn't want to admit it, the past few months at Glenn Avenue had been a bit easier. The shelters and transitional homes forced mother to straighten up. She was different for a little while, but it didn't last long. *It never does.* I think she secretly hated them as much as we did.

My last year in middle school, I was late every day because I had to make sure my siblings had breakfast. I would take them to school first and then walk with Piper to class.

I was thirteen years old and already a practical thief, stealing food from the local grocery store so Lillian and Parker wouldn't starve or cry "momma" to a woman who didn't even care. Most times, I found myself stealing the booklet of food stamps from her before she had the chance to sell it off to the highest bidder for "$.50 cents on the dollar." I always liked those booklets of money, they made me feel like an adult at the register. Tearing our one-dollar coupons and five-dollar coupons, I would smile to myself as I passed the bills across the register to the cashier.

For months on ends when the paper food coupons would run out, I would find myself filling my sleeves with more butter. "You can do this America," I'd tell myself as I took what Piper taught me and stuffed everything I could down my pants. By the end of each shopping trip, I would gain more than a few pounds of meat, cheese, and honey buns. Honey buns were my favorite treat. They looked as though someone took a book and smashed a cinnamon roll flat. They were perfectly frosted, oval shaped goodies I could devour in seconds. They reminded me of mother, I could always tell when she was in a good mood if she surprised me with a honey bun. She used to be happy and bring home treats for us, *But that was a long time ago. Honey buns are sooo good! I still love them!*

Somehow, the store employees never seemed to notice or care much about their job. Either that or they couldn't bear to stop the neglected little girl in aisle 6 from getting away with breakfast. Paranoid that I would get caught, I always made sure to never shop in the same store more than once a week, rotating locations frequently.

I spent so much time worrying about everyone else, taking care of everyone else and making sure everyone was safe and fed. Meanwhile, I had been failing nearly every subject in school. *I bet I could be a straight A student* - at least that's what I kept telling myself. I was a lot smarter than most kids my age, and I knew it. Maybe it was everything I had been through. As much as I loved school, going to class had been a drag most of the time. I was a bit more advanced than most kids. So much so, that it was too easy, and most subjects would bore me when I was there. I would find my mind wandering elsewhere, worrying about what seemed like more important things.

I was flunking out of school, but it wasn't because I didn't care. The first few months in that new house on Glenn, I landed myself in alternative school. I had missed so much class and failed to turn in so many assignments that they pulled me out of regular day and stuck me in the portables away from everyone else. Segregated, I was labeled a failure and bound to other rebellious teenagers that rolled blunts behind campus and fought each other every morning before class. School suddenly became less important, and eventually I lost interest in everything altogether. *I'm just not going there anymore. Don't they understand I was just too busy making sure Lillian and Parker were okay?*

Countless times mother's boyfriend Scott left our little faces swollen and bodies bruised. I tried to take the majority of the pain away from my siblings, tried desperately to put myself before them, diverting his aggression onto me so they would be safe. But we had all been so much smaller than him, and it was a losing battle. Scott had tainted what innocence there was left in us, but mother never cared because she loved him. *But what about us. Do you love us mother?* She put Scott above everyone and everything else, this tall, fresh-faced teenager that paid attention to her but beat her kids senseless.

It wasn't long until Parker began taking out his built-up frustrations and aggression on other children. He had been getting into a lot more fights at school, and the office always called me because they knew mother wouldn't answer.

Pretty quickly, I became acquainted with Parker's teachers at school. *I shouldn't have to do this!* He was continuously getting in trouble, and I couldn't control him. There were countless times I had gone to pick him up early because he was too much of a disruption or got suspended again. At first, I was actually shocked that they would let me walk off campus with him. Then again, we lived in the heart of an impoverished neighborhood that lacked resources and real supervision. So, it wasn't unheard of when no one ever questioned me, just shocking.

As for Lillian, I thought she might end up in the local bangers club down the street. Little mouthy girls who roamed the streets and fought everyone they possibly could. *Loud, obnoxious little brats they are! Always getting into trouble! Shitty little kids Ugh!* I tried my best to manage her friends, but it never ended well. Lillian was a wild one. As she got older, she developed a nasty mouth which got her into trouble a lot. Every time we went outside, I found myself slapping her around and yanking her by the hair, dragging her home and out of a fight. I knew that she hated being bossed around, but I didn't care.

"You ain't my momma!"

"I don't give a F-U mother-fucking C-K, Get home!"

When I wasn't dragging her around, she was regularly getting picked on. It took a while before I could convince the local hoodlums to stop jumping her.

"If anyone's going to hit my sister, it's gonna be me!" I yelled at them. After I tore through a few of the neighborhood brats, they eventually learned that big bad sister would come shred little kids if they continued to single her out.

"Let's go!" I'd scold her, pulling her off the ground and away from the kids down the street.

"It's not my fault! Nisha and I were minding our own business and they wanted to run up on us!"

"Bullshit, Lillian, you were out there looking for trouble! I told you to stay next to the house, you don't fuckin' listen."

"Well, we couldn't! There were a bunch of bitches at Mama Marks Park. I ain't staying there."

"Shut up."

After slapping her alongside her head, we would walk back to our house as she cried. Lillian and Parker ran wild and free, and no matter how much I tried to corral them, they couldn't be tamed. For a long time, I tried my best to stick to them like glue while they ran around outside but it was exhausting. I knew it was wrong to shake my fists at them, but for some reason, it was the only thing they responded to. Intimidation was the only thing that kept them out of trouble, real trouble.

I felt alone in this battle to keep Lillian and Parker safe and often thought about our eldest brother Bradley. I wondered what he was doing, or where he was. Did he miss us like we missed him? He stopped coming around after the military, and we didn't see him for a long time. *I bet he would know what to do about them.*

Every day at school was a struggle and half of the time I would never make it to school. One afternoon I sat next to Piper on the concrete staircase after the school bell rang, confiding in her.

"Dude, move in with me for good," She said.

"What do you mean move in for good?"

"I'm just saying, like… How much longer can you keep this shit up dude?"

"I don't know" I cried, placing my hands over my head as I curled up into a ball and melted on the staircase. *That would mean I'd have to leave Lillian and Parker behind for good this time.*

I knew that I couldn't say no, but it was a painful feeling for me to comprehend the fact that I would have to leave my siblings behind with that vile woman. I wouldn't be able to protect them or help them. As much as I worried about leaving them behind, I rejoiced in the fact that I would be free, completely free and away from her and that lifestyle. I could finally make my own mark in this world, and I wouldn't have to cry myself to sleep at night. *But what about my sister and brother?* A wave of guilt washed over me.

CHAPTER SIX

Wild as the Wind Blows

T he formation of the land began to change, and I knew I was getting closer to the city as the fog became denser, and the ground started to level out. The hills behind me seemed much further than they were just a moment ago, and I lost track of time as the white lines flew beneath my tires. Vivid memories of my siblings and I as children flashed through my head.

I didn't know if my siblings would miss me, I wondered what became of them. I hadn't seen them in such a long time, into adulthood my relationship with them was so rocky. After being separated for so long, it was difficult to reconnect with them and develop healthy relationships with each other. As much as we loved each other, we were all so vastly different. We were essentially strangers. At some point or another we all grew up broken in different ways and didn't know how to express ourselves or rekindle any type of positive relationship after what we had been through. We would never be normal, we could never just be…happy. We were off and on for years.

I wondered what they were doing at this exact moment as I drove through the mist. *Did they ever think about me? Did they miss me?* I wondered what they thought about me now. *What do they think when they look back on that day that I took them to play hide and seek in that abandoned building down the street from our childhood home? Did they think about all the fun we used to have there? Did they realize*

53

that we weren't just playing, but hiding from mother and all of her dirty secrets? A million unanswered questions spiraled through my mind looking for a place to settle. As I poured my heart into the drive ahead, memories of them flashed through my head while tears streamed down my face making it hard to distinguish the lines on the ground ahead of me. *This fog needs to clear up right now.*

As Piper and I sat on the staircase in the halls of our school, she looked at me solemnly and rubbed my back as I cried.

"America, you can't do this anymore. Come on, be real."

"I am fucking real, I'm really tired of this!" I told her.

"So just grab your stuff and bring it to my house, my mom is like, never home-she won't even care. Just move in with me."

I took a long time before I could tell Piper yes, but we both knew I had finally had enough. Once I finally made the decision to leave, I was excited. As I began my journey home, I could feel the energy build as I started to pick up the pace. I had been half running and skipping the entire way home. I was anxious to get the hell out of that house, but I didn't expect it to be as easy as it was. In fact, I was a bit intimidated by thoughts of how mother might react to me telling her I was leaving for good.

I quickly ran through the door and toward my bedroom yelling,

"Dana, I'm moving in with Piper."

"Ok" she hollered back.

I began packing my clothes, but curiosity led me back into the living room. I watched as she spun around in circles, intoxicated, dancing to the music that flowed from the stereo. She laughed loudly as music poured out all around her. I was shocked. *What, nothing? That's it? ok?* I could tell my last statement hadn't affected her, *did she even hear me?*

I hoped this wouldn't turn into a fight because I was exhausted, but if she insisted... then I was prepared to fight my way out of that door. *There is no way I'm staying here! I'd like to see her try and stop me. I'm done.* But in the end, she didn't care. I strode with confidence toward the front door, As I put my hand out to reach for the handle, I half expected her to stop me, but she only looked at me lovingly and waved goodbye. All the air escaped my lungs. I couldn't breathe. Tears began to fill the corners of my eyes as I trudged out the door with my little pack, *she's not going to see me cry. I won't give her the satisfaction of a single tear.* I ran out of the house angrily. "It's not like you care anyway!" I screamed, slamming the door behind me.

That moment played out so differently in my head. I had imagined that as I stepped through the door, she would call me back to wrap loving arms around me, and in a puddle of tears, she would beg me to stay. Promise to change. Tell me how different things were going to be, but that didn't happen. She let me walk out of her life all too easily, and that was the day she died to me. She wasn't my mother, and she hadn't been for a long time. When she gave up on me, I knew it was by choice. The men, the drugs, and the selfishness had overpowered her. I knew that I was alone in this world and had to learn how to fend for myself. I had stepped out of that home and into the wild at nearly thirteen years old. Walking down the street with Piper we began our venture into the new world.

The first few days without Lilian and Parker were truly difficult. I couldn't stop thinking about them.

"What if they are hurt? Or what if she doesn't feed them? Or what about that bitch down the street that keeps following Lillian"

I cried to Piper as we lay on her bed staring at the ceiling and dangling our toes above our head.

"Seriously, they are going to be fine, ok? They are so much older now, stop worrying about them."

"No, Lillian is just *barely* 10, and Parker will be 9 next year…they are still babies, dude."

Rolling her eyes, Piper said, "Yea well they don't act like babies, all they do is fight and talk shit."

"Easy for you to say. You don't know what it's like, you don't have any siblings!" I yelled at her.

"YES, I DO. They just don't live here. Now stop whining and let's go see what Victor is doing."

Piper had somehow managed to distract me with my newly found freedom. After a few days, I didn't have much time to think about them, but every so often I would come back home to visit my siblings for a few hours and check on them. Since mother never questioned my absence, it was easy to slip in and out.

Parker had been getting in more fights at school than usual, and Lillian... she just seemed to get mouthier, but I loved them both nonetheless. I knew they were troubled, as was I, but I couldn't be their protector any longer. I tried my best to make them understand why I left, but they were just too young. We were *all* too young and tied down with burdens far too heavy for such small children, but I was without a care in the world once I officially left home. It was wonderful. There was no other way of life except the one that I had dreamed of, and it was a beautiful dream. The possibility of a better life, knowing that things wouldn't always be terrible, kept me pushing forward.

The following year, Piper and I lived in a quaint little house on Santiago Way by ourselves. We tried our luck in high school, our freshman year at Grant High School was thrilling. Every day it was just the two of us roaming free and surviving the only way we knew how-with each other. Her mother was there occasionally when she wasn't high on meth, which to be honest wasn't often, so we spent the majority of our time alone. Since her mother was on Section 8, we never worried about rent or being evicted and everything was so immensely cheap that it was easy for her mother to maintain a stable home while continuing to dive head first into a world of addiction.

Nevertheless, I liked Piper's mom. She reminded me of my mother without all of the abuse and anger. She floated in and out of the house as she pleased, disappearing for days or weeks, but it never really mattered because Piper and I were used to fending for ourselves. For young girls barely hitting puberty, we somehow maintained life reasonably well.

A young couple down the street began befriending Piper, taking her to church every so often and inviting her for dinner. I tried to my best to stay away from them, I didn't like them at first and they only seemed to show interest in Piper. Some nights I attended youth gatherings with Piper because it was a nice change of pace, but I tried to maintain my distance. *If there is a god, then why all this pain? Why would he let us kids get hurt?* It just didn't make sense, but I went anyway because Piper enjoyed it, and everyone was so friendly there. For a long time, we both stayed far away from any kind of drugs or alcohol. We just knew better. It wasn't hard to imagine what kind of life lay down that path, and I wanted to be nothing like my mother.

"This is our life," I said, taking a razor and making a teeny slit on my palm. I passed the blade to Piper. Shaking our bleeding hands, we made a promise to never become like our parents, a blood pact which sealed our future.

For the majority of the time we spent together, we stole food when we were hungry, and our version of back to school clothes shopping was throwing on those same baggy sweatpants that fed our bellies and "trying on" a handful of items at the local thrift store. The fitting rooms were never monitored, and we would manage to make it home 10 lbs. heavier with change still in our pocket. We took what we needed and dreamed of things we never had.

We begged for money on the sidewalks and found neighbors that gave us cash for picking up their lawn or sweeping their porch. We made friends with the kids down the street and found families who'd feed us supper occasionally. There was once a time when Victor, Piper, and I would spend every waking moment together. From the break of dawn, till the sun went down. We led a life that felt to us, like childlike bliss, and I never seemed to notice how much we struggled. Life up until then was difficult, but the next few months with her were so comfortable that I relished in every moment.

I was without a worry in the world, I felt safe and far away from the life I had put behind me. Those were the good times, the first happy memories I was able to make as a kid. Piper and Victor were the first set of real friends I had ever had. I'll never forget the countless hours we spent soaring high into the sky on that trampoline at Victor's house. I loved watching as he would throw his little sister Carrie on the trampoline, her little body soaring up into the sky. We spent hours on that trampoline and day after day, swimming in their little three-foot-deep pool that stood in the backyard. We watched movies and played video games, rode bicycles around town, and finally felt like children.

We made friends with everyone we met. I'll never forget Victor's step-dad and the way he joked with us, he loved watching us all laugh, and he treated us like his children. He promised us we would always have a job at his construction company once we were old enough to drive. He said we would start in the office, scanning and copying things, but he died before we ever had the chance to grow up.

There were two little old ladies with a big empty house and lots of food to fill our bellies, and they even had bit of attic space for late night stargazing. The little old ladies let all the neighborhood children play in their house. They had a lovely tire swing in the backyard, and boxes filled with relics of the past and clothes for dress up and pretend. Victor, Piper and I would climb the ladder to their roof and lay up there for hours, gazing at stars from atop that 4-story house. It was just the three of us kids, and in that moment, that was all I needed. I felt so invincible up there, so far from everything and everyone. We promised each other that we would all remain friends forever, "Cross your heart and hope to die" as we interlocked pinkies and kissed the tips of our thumbs.

"It's sealed bitches, you can't take it back now," Piper exclaimed.

"I know, I know."

"Ya! Duh!" Victor said.

"Hey! Blood pact anyone?" I questioned jokingly.

"NO!" they yelled in tandem.

The ground below was such a distance from where we were on that roof! It seemed like light years away. With the stars just a little bit closer and the night within our grasp, the sky was at our fingertips. We spent hours on that roof trying to decipher the constellations and figure out the meaning of life. We giggled

---

and played on that rooftop countless times, and we didn't have to worry about anything except what we were going to do tomorrow.

In the months following, Piper and I we were like sisters and closer than any family I had known. Although we never had everything we needed, we made do and somehow found happiness where before there had been none.

"Ugh, I'm sooo hungry," Piper said as she threw a soft house slipper at my face. I dodged it, avoiding contact.

"Ya, me too, dude."

"Hey, do you think Victor's mom has any leftovers in her fridge?" she asked.

"Yeah right. If she does, Victor probably scarfed it by now," I said sarcastically.

"Let's go ask? No, wait…I have a better idea, put something on! We're going shopping."

We tossed our clothes on and threw our pajamas on the floor. We were gone and back in a blink of an eye with a can of biscuits, but not just *any* biscuits. The kind in a can that pops when you unravel it. Piper convinced me that we could make donuts at home with only a can of biscuits and some cooking oil.

"I swear, we can! My sister lives in New York, and she works at a donut store. It's so easy and practically the same thing, look!" she said, unveiling the dough from the cardboard mold.

As she squished together little balls of batter, and dropped them into the frying pan, I watched in amazement. We didn't need a fancy kitchen or a unique mixture to create a masterpiece. We used what little we had, and though starving, we had fun in the process. I was proud of our little creations. We roasted each donut in the hot oil for nearly a minute or so, just long enough to crisp and fluff as it turned into a delicious golden ball of crust. I shouted, "dude! That is so cool! Let's do it again!"

Piper and I had our good days and our bad. There were nights when we were afraid and would cry ourselves to sleep, and days where we went hungry, but we focused all that negative energy on other things to occupy our time. We painted our bedroom over and over again, splashing handprints onto the closet door promising to leave it there forever as we signed our name below each hand. We created happiness out of thin air and invested the majority of our time into things like art and figure skating.

We spent so many hot summer days in that old ice skating rink down the street, before it burned down. Every spare dollar we had we invested into time at that local rink. We saved as much as we could, but it was rare when we could actually buy our way into Iceland. Rentals and sessions were so expensive, so most of the time we just sat in the bleachers laughing and giggling, watching skilled performers practice their melancholy dance on the ice before us.

We watched and learned by observing and getting to know everyone in that little rink on Del Paso. We made friends with a few of the people who worked there, and they would allow us admission when their manager wasn't looking. When we did have the chance to skate, it was the highlight of my week. Sliding across that frozen canvas was like magic. I could feel the happiness spill into the atmosphere as I would glide over the ice. I lived for the little moments and dreamt of bigger ones to come. I was going to become something one day, maybe even a figure skater. *I'm going to skate for Disney!*

CHAPTER SEVEN

Cool Watermelon Sunday's

My fingers folded tightly around the steering wheel as I snapped back into reality. I was so tired of running from my past. An ongoing pain lingered in the back of my mind on a daily basis, and I just wanted the memories to fade. As much as I enjoyed thinking about the times that made me smile, I still wanted desperately to forget them. As I slid the window down again and inhaled the salty air, the car began to slow.

I was suffocating, and I needed to get out. Maneuvering onto the side of the road once again, I pulled the car to a stop and got out, kicking the dirt and screaming at a god who never listened. I cursed the world and yelled at people like a maniac as they drove by. My legs buckled, and my knees hit the dirt as I swallowed clouds of dust. I sat down and placed my hands over my head, trying to understand all of the memories that never seemed to stop flooding in.

I wanted to rip my heart from beneath my ribs and crush it in my fist, watching it crumble to the dirt below. I wanted to forget my siblings, my friends, my old life. I wanted to forget that I ever tried to adopt Jordan's niece, *my niece*. I thought I could help her. I thought Jordan and I could give her a life that her mother couldn't. I wanted to save her like no one had saved me.

"But we just fucked that up! Just like everything else we did together!" I screamed into the oblivion on the side of the road.

—

I've really gotta get to the beach. Am I almost there? As images of Kaycee's face floated into my head, I climbed back into the car.

"I'm flying momma, look!" Kaycee would say. I was twenty-four years old. My girls, Kaycee and Lilah, were just learning how to ride, and it was literally impossible for us all to ride together, so instead Jordan and I walked them in circles around the block until they were panting and out of breath. Sometimes they would jump off of their bikes, and their stubby little toddler legs would push the tricycles as fast as they could, wobbling down the street next to us.

Their legs were so tiny compared to the training wheels my girls tried so hard to spin. Kaycee tried her best to speed down the street as fast as she could, but she never made it far. Giggling, I would pick up my pace to walk next her. It was always a walk though, I never had to run. Her idea of "fast" was adorable, and I loved every minute of it.

It was always sunny on those soft summer streets downtown, and everything seemed permanently bathed in near perfect light. The trees glittered in the air above as the leaves trembled in the sunlight, it was breathtaking. Sporadic beams of light fell down upon us as we played in the Downtown streets. Lilah's perfect brown curls blew in the wind and Kaycee's eyes shone with happiness as the four of us raced barefoot down the sidewalk.

Summer was always like that, barefoot. When we were fostering our niece, our days were filled with wild chalk drawings that stretched nearly the entire sidewalk on our block, and watermelon Sunday's. *Those were the best!* I would bring their little pink princess table outside and place it on the porch with plates of sliced watermelon, and the girls and I would sit outside for hours and devour endless mounds of watermelon. Their tiny round cheeks were full of laughter as I indulged them in childlike conversations about their perfect Disney princess and their favorite toys. It was innocent and nearly as sweet as the watermelon we had between our teeth.

CHAPTER EIGHT

Is There Anyone There?

E ven the happy memories from adulthood were too sad to linger in because I knew she was gone, and I would probably never see her again. My darling daughter, my baby girly. *My niece, my Kaycee baby! I promise we were going to adopt you. I tried so hard to keep it together for you, I failed.* I called out to her as though she were sitting there in the car beside me. I tried my best to keep our little family together, but at the end of each day, there was a toxic mass that swirled like a black hole inside my heart and stole the beauty out of everything that resembled happiness. It sucked the life out of our marriage, and it sucked the soul right out of me.

Kaycee had been tossed around the system for years before we were able to foster her. At the time, our daughter Lilah had been four years old, just a bit younger than Kaycee. At first everything seemed to be going well, until it didn't. Aside from Jordan's wicked and overbearing family blaming our relationship for their failures, our marriage was falling apart. I was broken and the anger and resentment I held onto was destroying everything I loved and held dear. When it was evident that we couldn't help Kaycee anymore, Jordan and I stopped the adoption process in hopes of giving Kaycee a fresh start at a new life. We couldn't be the parents she needed, especially not in the environment we were in. We couldn't save her, I couldn't even save myself.

—

After taking a long, deep breath and a few minutes to rest, I started the car engine. Driving further into the oblivion. For a moment, as emotionally drained as I was, I was okay because I knew that I loved both girls fiercely. I also knew that Kaycee was in a better home. Even if it broke my heart, I knew she was okay, and it was the love that I had for her that allowed me to give her away. It was the kind of love I had always wanted but never had. With my hand wrapped around the steering wheel, I turned on the radio and smiled, because as dark as my emotions were right then, I knew that Jordan could never take that love away from me, not even in death. *I used to be a great mother, I hope they'll remember me that way.* As I drove across the bay bridge and into an unfamiliar city, I sighed. *Oh my god, I'm here. Hello, San Francisco.*

"Mrs. Barren, my brother, and sister need help… I just. I-I-I just can't" I cried.

"It's okay America," Piper said patting the top of my hands as she placed her hands over mine.

Mrs. Barren was my 9th-grade art teacher, the only teacher whom I had ever connected with. She was a brilliant artist, and her voice was gentle and soothing. Whenever she spoke, I somehow felt like I was home. I used to imagine what it would be like to be her daughter. I imagined she was the kind of mom who helped with homework and baked homemade apple pies with an apron. *I bet she was a great mom.* She was the only teacher who ever pushed me to recognize my own talent.

"Has anyone ever told you what an amazing artist you are? Can you paint me something please?'

And I did. I spent as much time as I could in her class, mixing mediums and blending charcoal. She gave me freedom to express myself through art and let Piper and I roam the halls, sketching images of inanimate objects, or students as they sifted through their lockers wasting time between classes. She gave us freedom with an attached responsibility, to bring back a completed sketch or picture.

In her class, I wasn't ashamed to share my talent with the world, but I felt loosely connected to my mother. I hated that we both shared an artistic background, and it always prevented me from indulging in painting until Mrs. Barren began pushing me. I could tell she believed in me, especially when my drawings would end up on her wall or hanging near the whiteboard for everyone to see. It made me feel special, and I really needed that. I decided to stay after class one day, to ask for help because I didn't know what else to do.

"You can tell her," Piper urged as she continued to clasp my hand tightly within hers. Mrs. Barren listened patiently to me as I drained my heart on the classroom floor. Things were getting more difficult than Piper and I could manage. Scott had been leaving bruises on Lillian and Parker more often. I hadn't been around as much but whenever I visited, I could tell things were progressively getting worse, especially since mother would usually be intoxicated and passed out. Some days I would walk into the house and find her slouched over the kitchen table or balled up in a fetal position on the floor while Lillian and Parker cried endlessly in the back bedroom.

"Is that why you've been late to class?" Mrs. Barren asked,

"Yes. I have to leave Piper's house really early and walk to my mother's house in time to walk my sister and brother to school, and if I don't bring them breakfast in the morning, then mother won't feed them all day and they call me crying" I sobbed.

Parker would give me report cards monthly and I would scribble away a parent signature. "Students absences are affecting grade work" "Student continues to be disruptive in class" "Student is repeatedly sent to the principal's office for fighting at recess."

"Sometimes, Mrs. Barren, I just want to go to school too! I can't always be there."

With tears welling in her eyes, she pulled me from Piper's grasp and held me tight. "Alright girls, I want you to come with me, and I want you both to talk to the principal okay? Can you do that for me?" Piper and I both nodded our heads and trailed behind Mrs. Barren until we reached the principal's office.

When the principal finally called us into his office, we sat there and told him tidbits of everything that had been going on. Without much of an expression, he took a deep breath and told us a matter of factly, "We are going to call someone special to take you to a safe house while we get this all straightened out okay?"

"Well, what does that mean?" Piper inquired.

"It's a place full of children like yourselves that just need a safe home to sleep for a while, someone to talk to, and maybe some good food. Sound good?" he smiled enthusiastically.

Piper was full of questions, asking what color the sheets were, to how many other kids there were to who owned the house, and many other things that the principal promised we would get the answers to once we arrived.

Within twenty minutes a tall, strange brunette in a sleek navy-blue suit showed up to drive us away. We climbed into the backseat of her car and she drove us to a large house hidden behind a wall of bushes. The driveway on the property was long and paved with dirt. At the end of the driveway stood the building that we were going to live in for the next few weeks.

"Wow, where are we?" Piper wondered aloud. I tightly clasped the strap on my backpack and stepped through the front door, legs shaking. Walking past the entryway and following the lady in the suit, we stepped into the dining room. A simple yet elegant table stood before us with neatly stacked dishes and silverware. Two older boys were rearranging the plates and preparing for an early supper, hardly paying attention to us.

Looking around, I was entranced by the room that we were standing in. It felt warm and tranquil. It was the complete opposite of anything I was used to. The walls were decorated with random abstract pieces of art, and the floor was softened with a big colorful throw rug that felt squishy underfoot. On either side of us were two halls that led into the bedrooms. The living room was tucked away in a little corner to our right, where 3 children gathered around clutching controllers in their hands, fixated on the TV screen. "Well hello, ladies!" a stranger announced, stepping in the room with us.

"First things first! Let's go over the rules."

Her voice was too high pitched and cheery for my mood. Staring at her perfectly white teeth, I wanted to scream, "Just get it over with!" She kept talking and talking, for what seemed like an eternity. Only half listening, the only thing I picked up on was something about sharing, cleaning, and bedtime. Her lips were moving faster than I could keep up with and her smile was so distracting. *Ugh, please stop talking.*

"Are you ready?" the strange woman said. Piper and I both looked at each other momentarily. Shrugging, we took a left and followed her down the dimly lit hall toward our new bedroom. "This side of the house is for girls only. Boys sleep on the other side of the house, and our office is just down that way," she said pointing in the direction we just came from. "Now I don't want you ladies sneaking out after curfew okay?

"Okay," we both said in tandem.

The bedroom was bare except for two sets of bunk beds that were pushed up against opposing walls to our right. The hard tile floor was glazed with a clear gloss that made it look slippery next to the wooden beds. Directly in front of us, there was a sliding glass door without curtains. *Great.*

"It so empty in here," Piper whispered.

"Yeah, what the hell happened to the rest of the decorations in here? Why isn't it all warm and fuzzy in here?" I asked her bluntly.

Laughing, the woman shrugged off my inquisition, urging us to pick a bed and follow her back down the hall. Soon after, we were supplied with clean clothes, a toothbrush, and colorful socks that wrapped around each toe, hugging them tightly.

"Once you're finished dressing, report to the kitchen and help us prepare for dinner."

"But I don't know how to prepare a dinner like that,"

"I don't know how to prepare a table" Piper chimed.

"Don't worry, you'll both catch on quick here."

Our first night was uncomfortable, though it started off well. I was quiet as we all sat down at the table for supper. I couldn't remember the last time I had a real meal like this. There were mashed potatoes, corn, fried chicken, and perfectly crisp french fries. The biscuits were soft and layered with melting butter, breaking off piece by piece. My body shuddered at how good each piece felt in my mouth.

Bowls were clattering, and hands were reaching across the table in all directions as the children picked and pulled at the variety of food on the table. Everyone mostly kept to themselves, which I liked because I was not ready to have a conversation with anyone. They were careful not to ask too many questions and left us alone for the most part. Once supper was finished, a few children headed straight for the living room where a variety of video games and electronic devices waited for us to use. Everything about this house seemed so odd. *Where did all these kids come from?*

"Hey, do you think Lillian and Parker are coming here too?" I asked Piper.

"I don't know… I don't see anyone little kids here."

Making our way back toward the bedroom we had been introduced to earlier, we decided to stay in our room for the rest of the night. The first night was terrifying. Staff members walked the premise at night and peeked in at us while we slept. I could hear the creaking sound of the door as they periodically opened and shut it throughout the night.

It took a few weeks before I was able to feel at ease and make friends at the safe house, but I tried to keep my distance because I never knew when someone new would arrive or someone would be leaving. Chores were always done before we were allowed to play video games or run around outside in the backyard. Staff members worked around the clock, switching shifts every 8 hours, making sure there was always someone awake. We were never alone.

Every so often in the middle of the night, Piper and I would tiptoe down the hallway and stand next to the office door, listening to the adults' gossip about their lives before quickly running back to our room to giggle.

The children ranged broadly in ages. Some were younger, twelve maybe thirteen, while others were in their later years and almost adults. We were comfortable for a few weeks, sweeping the dining hall and helping prepare dinner with the kitchen staff. We drew pictures and gossiped about the cute older boys across the hall. We felt safe until the day the police arrived on our porch with my biological father.

CHAPTER NINE

Safety is Overrated

The city was glorious. People roamed the streets bundled in scarves and beanies. Intersections moved quickly as trolleys rolled around chiming. The buildings huddled close together, and everyone around me walked with purpose, I loved it. The sky was darkened with thick fog that made it difficult to see the top of most of the buildings. I wandered the streets aimlessly searching for the nearest liquor store-*alcohol would make it less painful, right?*

"Do you know where I can find a convenience store?" I attempted to ask a stranger on the sidewalk before being hastily ignored and shoved past. *Rude.* I knew that I must look ridiculous because everyone refused to acknowledge me. My face was swollen and my heart was full, the aftermath of a long, bitter car ride. Looking at my reflection in a car window, I reminded myself of my mother, a frazzled torn, mess of a person. No wonder everyone shoved past me, I looked like I was coming down from a seven-day binge. My sullen eyes were red and sunken into my face. My hair was ragged, windblown, and tangled from the fight with Jordan a few hours before.

I used my hands to flatten the top of my hair the best I could, wiping away remnants of the dust cloud I had submerged myself in a few miles back. I half smiled at myself in the reflection without really knowing why and hopped back in my car, randomly driving through city streets alone. *Good enough.*

"America! please come here!"

I heard a loud voice call out. Piper and I ran toward the sound, giggling and stumbling into the dining hall where two police officers stood. My heart began to race as I glanced over at Piper.

"What's going on?" I asked.

Almost as if she knew something terrible was going to happen, Piper placed her hand within mine and squeezed firmly.

"We are taking you home, kid," the dark-haired officer stated firmly.

"What? What do you mean home?! I can't go home! I don't live there anymore! I'm not going anywhere with you!"

Piper began sobbing uncontrollably as two offices took me by the shoulders and pulled me outside where my estranged father, Esteban, stood waiting. *Oh no, ... please no.*

"No no no! Take me home to Dana's house! I want to go there. Take me there! I don't know this man!" I screamed, pulling at the officer's jacket.

"Mija, come on, it's ok," Esteban said soothingly.

"Fuck you!" I said, kicking a pile of dirt at him before the officers stuffed me in the backseat of his truck.

Piper, crying hysterically in the background, was forced back into the safehouse by a staff member, as what seemed to her like a stranger and his wife drove me away.

That night, I knew I needed to escape and find my brother and sister. It had been weeks since I'd heard a thing about them, but I was so exhausted once my face hit the pillow in this strange new room, my eyes closed, and my thoughts went silent.

The next morning, I awoke earlier than everyone else and prepared to escape. These people weren't my family, and I wasn't staying here no matter what that policeman said. *Screw this.* Puncturing the screen and tearing it straight down the middle of his daughter's bedroom window, I slid out and darted through the city as fast as I could, back to the little house on Glenn Avenue where I had last seen Lilian and Parker just a few weeks prior.

Standing in the doorway, staring at mother with tears welling in my eyes, I could tell that the conversation with her was going nowhere. She was too distracted with the little specks on the wall to even fully understand what she had done, upon first glance I knew that she was high.

"Dana, where are they?!"

"I dunno, gone with their dad."

"What do you mean, gone?" I screamed "Where are they?!"

"Somewhere in Oregon with their father. Now stop screaming or they will hear you!"

"Who is they?! Dana, Listen! Look at me! Dana, D-A-N-A" I screamed, tearing at my hair.

During our stay at the safe house, child protective services intervened on my siblings' behalf, following up on an emergency report. Mother must have known that they were going to rip Lillian and Parker away from her, and she couldn't afford to go to jail or be held accountable for the kids. Too much abuse and neglect had swept through that little house on Glenn Avenue and she was worried, but not about the drugs or drinking. She was a great deceiver and could easily pass any drug test they placed before her as long as she timed it all right. She was great at figuring out how long it would take for the drugs to run out of her system if she drank enough water or took the right amount of cleansing pills. Hell, if that didn't work, she would just borrow someone else's urine, so she wasn't worried about any of that.

What she really worried about was the way they looked, how they acted and behaved. She wanted to hide her bruised, broken and starved children, and the fact was that her nineteen-year-old boyfriend had been beating them, manipulating them, and touching them in all the wrong ways. So, she decided to call their father and get rid of them before anyone could seek the truth. Lillian and Parker shared the same father, but much like myself, never had much contact with him because he lived in another state. He was just another stranger they saw every few years.

"I was trying to protect them!" She said, with her alcohol infused words and messy hair. The bruises on her arm and partial black eye indicated a fight the night before with Scott. She shifted constantly side to side as though she was looking for something that wasn't there. Her paranoia had regularly made me second guess life, people, and places. I never felt secure with her. Was someone coming after us? Are we really okay at night, What did she get us into this time? I was always worried and fearful, yet strong when I needed to be.

My mother instilled a never-ending doubt within me at such a young age that I wasn't sure I would be able to bounce back from it. She tainted my soul with only the darkest of emotions. When I lost Lilian and Parker, and Bradley was nowhere to be seen, I knew I didn't have anyone left. I just wish I could have said goodbye.

CHAPTER TEN

Eres un Gringa

few blocks into my adventure, I stumbled across a liquor store. I parked hastily and walked inside with a mission. Get alcohol. Get out, Find water. Making my way through the crowded aisles, I located the fridge in the back and pulled open the door. I stood there indecisively, staring at all of the beautiful colored bottles. Green, blue, and clear glass bottles lined the shelves, each representing a different flavor. *I don't want this fru-fru filler…ugh.* Letting go of the handle, I walked to the cashier empty-handed. "Can I have a fifth of Morgan, please?" I watched as the old man spun around and pulled a bottle from the top shelf. He scanned the bottom and began to wrap the container in a paper bag.

"Can I see your ID?" he asked.

"Sure." I fumbled through my purse and flipped through various pockets in my wallet but I couldn't find it. *Seriously? This is really happening right now?* My ID just wasn't there.

"I am so sorry, I seemed to have misplaced it… I was born in 1990 if that helps any?" I knew full well that nothing I could say would convince this man to let me walk out of there with alcohol. His face was smug as he placed his hands on his hip and said, "No ID, no alcohol."

"I drove here from Sacramento, it's not like I can just drive back and get it. Please?" I begged. He shook his head

"Ugh, ridiculous" I mumbled in frustration as I turned away and shoved through the front door.

"This day could literally not get any worse, Fuck it! I can die without alcohol!" I yelled dramatically as I threw my hands in the air and marched toward the silver hunk of metal that I had left parked in the 7-Eleven parking lot across the street. I contemplated whether or not I wanted to try my luck there but decided against another embarrassing moment. I hate uncomfortable situations. *Nope, not happening again.* I slid my key into the door and propped it open, then began shoving my hands in all the nooks and crannies of my car, looking for my ID. *Maybe I dropped it somewhere.*

Within a few minutes, I had torn through the entire contents of my car and wound up with 2 bags off half-eaten gummy bears, three french fries, 68 cents in change, an old parking ticket, and my favorite book, each page folded in a mysterious manner, courtesy of a 5-year-old. Clearly, my ID was not there. As I sat on the edge of my seat with my hands covering my face, I let my feet dangle outside. The thick smell of fresh seawater filled my car as I fell into another clouded memory.

"You don't deserve a bed, you can sleep on the ground until you earn a bed" Esteban would say. He took away anything and everything he considered a privilege. I was never allowed to call anyone or touch a phone to call Lilian and Parker. There were even days he refused to take me to school as a form of punishment. There were many senseless and cruel punishments that always seemed to leave me feeling worthless.

He was a vile man, my father. Filled with hate, unspeakable rage, and racial prejudice that most people didn't see. In fact, to everyone else, he seemed like a pretty decent guy I'm sure. I'm sure everyone saw him as strict, perhaps, but loving and kind nonetheless. What they didn't know was that he had a sly way of manipulating people and making them believe he was innocent regardless of the situation. He was a master deceiver.

"Gringa," he'd call me-white girl. "You're going to be just like your mother when you grow up." He spewed.

I hated him for it, I boiled with anger, but I learned to keep my emotions contained in fear of the repercussions. There were some days I tried my best to ignore him and make a solid attempt at getting along with my half-sister and his wife. It always seemed to make him happy when I would "straighten up" around his family and keep my mouth closed about the late-night visits in my bedroom.

I didn't know my relatives very well. I had met them a few times when I was younger, but my father never stayed in the picture. I had only met him a handful of times and each time, I refused to visit him.

His family was large! At gatherings, there were always other children my age that I enjoyed running amuck with, and he would let me, as long as I had behaved the day before. I grew used to visiting my cousins and eventually looked forward to it, so I made sure to do everything in my power to listen to him, if only to escape for a fraction of time at Aubela's house. His family was beautiful. They gave me something to look forward to when things were difficult.

"We're going to visit Abuela. And keep your mouth shut!" he would say in his heavy Spanish accent, shaking a finger at me.

Sometimes he forced my half-sister Giselle and I to play the kissing game. Obediently, we sat on either side of him on the living room couch. He would place his hands on our buttocks and squeeze firmly. Then, we would hastily try to put our lips on his cheeks, but he would shake his head back and forth between Giselle and I, attempting to catch our mouths with his. Every so often he slid his tongue between my lips. I played his games to be a "good little girl." I was afraid that if I didn't play along, he would beat me behind closed doors. Esteban was much stronger and bigger than any boyfriend mother had, I couldn't defend myself. So, I did whatever it took to go to Abuela's house.

Abuela's house was always filled with family and friends, games of "Loteria," and "pozole con tortas y tostadas." Those were the days I could escape him, and things were okay because I felt somewhat normal running around with other children.

I would listen to my uncles tell scary stories and let my "Tia Lorie" weave my hair into a long braid as all the children sat around talking and laughing. He didn't hurt me at Abuela's house, and when we visited Tia Lorie, I would bask in her loving presence. She always made me feel like one of her children while Giselle and I ran around her backyard splashing in the pool with cousins. I loved their family. A piece of me wanted to tell them how much their sweet Esteban was hurting me, but at the same time, I didn't want them to look at me differently. I didn't want to be cast out, and I wasn't sure if they would believe me if I said anything anyways. The few times I disobeyed Esteban, he left me trembling on the floor. At school, friends had begun noticing the bruises, and I was coaxed into telling my dirty little secret to the school counselor. Once social services became involved in my life again, I thought they would save me. They promised me that no matter what I said, they would make sure nothing bad would ever happen. They lied.

I told them about Giselle and the nights that she would sleep in bed naked with him, and they "investigated," but somehow, he managed to keep me in his care. He convinced them I was lying, a rebellious pre-teen, and with his wife and daughter by his side they were convinced I had fabricated the whole story. He had told the social worker that Giselle wet the bed regularly, forcing him to undress her, and so they would just toss her back in bed with them until they could change the sheets the next morning. He told them I had a "difficult upbringing" and caused the bruises myself. But he never told them about the day after, when he would spoil Giselle, taking her shopping for shoes, clothes, toys, anything she wanted. Of course, she had to be a "good little girl" first. Giselle was an impressionable young mind and quite a few years younger than I was, so it wasn't difficult to coax her into saying whatever he wanted, especially if it meant she got a new toy. "Ahh, mi Princesa" he would say, as they walked hand in hand in the store, Giselle bouncing around joyously while I was forced to walk five feet behind their footsteps "where I belonged."

I didn't want to play his games anymore. As the months went on and my body began to develop more, he would start cupping his hands around my breast as I walked by. After a while, I couldn't take the abuse anymore. I began running away for days at a time, making my way across town to grandmother's house, or to old neighborhood friends that always took me in. Every day was challenging while I was away, but I found comfort in knowing that at least I wasn't there with him.

CHAPTER ELEVEN

On the Bathroom Floor

Three cans fell from a grocery bag as the stranger beside me opened the door to his white pickup truck. The clatter of the metal smashing against the concrete instantly caught my attention. Shaking my head and focusing my eyes on the old man, I snapped back into my surroundings. I could see the frustration spread across his face as he bent over to pick up the cans.

"Here let me help you," I said, handing him sliced green beans and a few other random veggies.

"Thanks," he replied.

"No problem" I sighed loudly.

"What are you doing out here sitting like that miss? Something wrong?" he said,

Is something wrong? IS SOMETHING WRONG?!

"No, I'm fine. I'm just..."

"You don't look so good"

"It's been a rough day, I'm not from here...long story."

"Well, I'm sorry to bother you. Have a good day."

"Wait! No! Can you please... I'm sorry. This is going to sound completely crazy, but do you think that if I gave you cash, that you could maybe buy me alcohol?"

Shocked the gentleman looked at me in disbelief, his eye widened with curiosity, and his body stood a bit straighter than it was before. "Excuse me?" he said. "How old are you?"

As we stood there chatting momentarily, he began questioning me further, after some time and with a bit of hesitation, he finally said yes. As I placed the paper bills into his palm, he tilted his head slightly to the side and paused, "Are you sure that you're over 21? You look pretty young miss?"

Smiling, I reassured him that I had merely lost my ID and wanted to enjoy the beach with a small drink.

As I waited in the car, tearing at my nails with my teeth, I half expected this stranger to come out empty handed. *Good Job, America. He's just going to take the money and run.*

But he didn't. Eventually the tall grey-haired man came out of the store, walked toward me and tapped on my window.

"Thank you so much!" I shouted. "No problem miss. Now be safe and don't go too close to the water," he insisted.

Ha! Okay. Turning my key in the ignition, I made my way back to the busy streets of San Francisco once again. A few blocks down I pulled into a large parking lot near Ocean Beach and paused momentarily. Amazed at the immensity of the shimmering water below the hill, I gazed past the coastline and out into the open sea. *I made it.*

"Get out of the bathroom America! " Gloria screamed from the kitchen, "It's time to eat."

I ignored her attempts to get my attention while I lay on the bathroom floor cuddling the base of the toilet. *Who cares?* Food was the last thing on my mind as I hovered over the toilet every five minutes, heaving piles of yellow liquid into the basin. Something wasn't right, and I knew it deep down, but I didn't have the energy to convince Esteban to take me to the hospital.

Even if I tried, I doubted he would care. I'd been in the bathroom for hours, and they had ignored me earlier when I told them I didn't feel well.

It had been two days since I could keep anything down, and I couldn't remember the last time I had anything to drink, yet somehow my body kept producing streams of yellow bile liquid that burned the lining of my throat and the outer edges of my lips as it poured out and into the toilet. *Something's not right.*

"Dammit, America! This is the last time I'm going to tell you to get *out* of the bathroom, I know you're faking it!" Gloria screamed. "Just send her back to her mom," Gloria told my father.

"Fine, starving all weekend it is." He said.

I could hear them whispering from beneath the door. As I lay quiet, I knew my energy was slowly fading. Weak and unable to move any more, I closed my eyes and put my head to rest on the bathroom floor. My body jolting up every few minutes to produce violent bursts of vomit on the floor all around me, seeping into my hair and sticking to my cheek while I lay there.

Sometime later, Esteban managed to unlock the door and peered inside at my motionless body. As my gaze met his, I watched his frustration over the locked door fade as a glimmer of something I hadn't seen before appeared: He was worried.

"Vamonos. We are going to the hospital."

Plucking me from the floor, he took me through the living room and outside to his little red truck. Gloria scurried behind us with bags of fruit and a couple of drinks for the drive. Pulling a seatbelt over my shoulder, she slammed the door shut as I melted into the soft cushion. I always hated that obnoxiously loud truck and the way it roared like a diesel that was three bolts short of falling apart or losing a tire. The tacky bold white letters

—

plastered to the side of the truck gave people hope that Mr. Fixer could repair their plumbing needs -Esteban could fix anything! *Yea right.* The vomiting continued until the doctors strapped me to a gurney and stuck a needle in my vein. My temperature was so high I began to lose sensation in my fingers and my body was hot to the touch. My shaking legs sent chills sputtering down my spine.

After a while, I knew the medicine was working because for the first time in days I felt comfortable laying down. Esteban left the room just as the doctor began sticking my spine with a needle. They told me to curl my body and hold my knees tightly against my chest, "And don't move, because even the slightest error could paralyze you." the doctor said. The pain from the puncture knocked me out. The nurse near my bedside rubbed my arm as I lost consciousness.

I awoke sometime later lying flat in my bed with my eyes closed. Slowly I began to absorb the environment around me. I overheard the doctor telling the nurse he needed a signature to admit me, but I had been abandoned.

"She doesn't have anyone here doctor. I tried to get a hold of her mother but no one's answering."

"Alright then, just get her upstairs. We'll figure it out."

As my eyes fluttered open and I tried to adjust to the blinding lights, a man emerged from behind the curtain. "Do you know your fathers phone number sweetie?" he asked. I groggily rattled off the number and sometime later found myself in a room a few floors up. In the children's ward, I didn't see my father for a few weeks after that day.

Upstairs, I had my own bedroom. They admitted me to the children's department so that my body could recover from viral meningitis. I spent the next few weeks in a hospital bed watching re-runs of Lizzie McGuire and playing video games from beneath the sheets. TVs were mounted to the walls alongside stickers of butterflies and animals in assorted colors. The room was vibrant, comforting even.

A little while after they moved me to the children's ward, Mother came in for a moment holding a stuffed bear. I was shocked to see her, it had been so long. She told me that she was back in the shelters. "But don't worry! I'll be out of there in no time!" she said. *Yea right.*

After mother-Dana disappeared, It was days before I saw another face I recognized. My eyes were closed when she arrived. Her footsteps were soft, and I could hardly hear her move about my room. A woman in hospital scrubs cleaned and made little adjustments to my collection of video games. Opening my eyes, I could tell she looked familiar.

"Do you remember who I am?" she asked sweetly as she lay a colorful crocheted blanket atop my body.

"Amanda," I whispered, slowly sitting up.

"That's right" she smiled.

Bradley's father had remarried Amanda after divorcing mother. I had met her a few times when she picked up or dropped Bradley, and she was always kind. She sat there chatting with me for a while, asking questions and talking about my brother Bradley.

Amanda and I talked a few times a week after that. She told me that her job was to make children feel comfortable while they stayed at the hospital. It didn't make sense to me, but I never questioned it because I didn't want her to leave like everyone else had. She would play games with me for hours and introduce me to new activities. I tried to make friends once I began to regain my strength, but most of the other children that wandered the halls were quiet and didn't speak, except one little girl who

—

couldn't have been much younger than I was. Her cheeks were thin, and her body was pale. She was missing an entire head of hair, but she smiled with a fierceness that lit up the room.

"Why are you here? I asked her.

"I'm sick," she replied. Was it contagious like mine? How did she get it? I wanted to know, but I didn't ask her.

"I'm sorry." I whispered to her.

"It's okay. Daddy says I'm going to visit the angels. I know he's going to miss me so much when I die, but it's okay," she told me softly.

Questions flooded my mind. *What? What did she just say? Why? How?* It bothered me that she was dying and yet it seemed so natural to her. I didn't like that she had come to terms with this fact. I just couldn't understand why she was so perfectly content when she told me. We sat in the common room together and sifted through bins, smiling at one another. After a while I stopped seeing her in the little corner where toys and games filled the shelves. I wandered in there every so often to look for her, but she had vanished, so I spent the remainder of my time in my room devouring hot plates of tasty food.

I wasn't used to all of this attention, nor was I ready to leave the hospital. When they told me I would be okay, I wanted to stay there. I wasn't prepared to go back to Esteban's house.

CHAPTER TWELVE

Is it Over?

My body sunk into the ground below me with each step I took, and a sense of security washed over me, I felt at home. Softly my feet pressed into the sand beneath my toes as I made my way toward the water, away from the world, and toward the emptiness of the ocean that spread out endlessly before me. I found solace near a little stack of rocks that lined the shore a few hundred feet from where I parked my car. Near the edge of the ocean, I could see freight ships slowly passing by as they kissed the horizon and swept past me. I stood there staring into the distance for a moment before the sheer vastness of it all sent me to my knees, a sobbing mess.

As wave after wave crawled across the tan canvas and toward me, I inhaled the ocean's beauty. Every moment was breathtaking as I sat before this enormous body of water, watching it swell and pour onto the shoreline with never-ending intensity. Savoring every moment, I let the cool breeze sift through my hair, and reaching my hands high into the sky above, I stretched my arms wide and surrendered my heart to the sea. Oddly enough, staring out into that open water made all of the problems I'd ever had seem so minuscule compared to the mass amount of water that lay before me. I felt so small, so fragile and so perfectly content looking into the distance, looking at nothing really. As the wind ruffled my hair and my arms descended, each wave swept away a little more of my past as I became absorbed in the sheer vastness of it all.

The water extended for miles toward the skyline, painting a pastel grey scene before me. You might expect the water to have been blue, but it seemed a deeper gray more than anything. Perhaps it was the time of day and the angle of the sun that affected the color. The waves seemed to have a personality, moving in every direction with no specific order, they reminded me of how life is: random. I was memorized by that sea for hours. The way the water was moving looked as though someone was digging their hands into the depths of the sea and pulling the water upward from below, pushing everything to the surface.

It looked like the ocean was cleansing itself, exposing all of its imperfections as I watched the waves hit the sand below me. Tiny shells, seaweed, and remnants of what once rested on the ocean floor were scattered across the sand before me. What was once a glorious sea urchin free-floating underwater, was now a lifeless shell. As the swells rose and crashed back down, folding over themselves, the water seemed nearly transparent. Walking closer to the shoreline, I tossed my bag aside and skipped across broken shells and crystal-clear rocks the size of a penny. I lay on the ground parallel to the crashing waves, staring at the water as it crawled toward me and appeared to slowly simmer away, I cried. Stagnant on the shoreline, I let the cold water fill the empty space around my body and soak me until I could no longer feel the tips of my fingers and toes.

Freezing, I jumped up and collected my things, walked toward a flat rock that rested near the ocean and plopped down. As I nestled into place, I opened the brown paper bag and my hand began to shake. Frustrated and unable to keep the drink still, I started clawing furiously at the top of the cap until it spun off abruptly and fell to the ground. Tossing my head back, I pressed the cold glass against my lips, pouring nearly half of the contents down my throat and into my belly. Within minutes I could feel the world spinning around me. *Too much, too quick, oh shit.*

As my body began to feel light, the pounding in my head ceased, and I slowly leaned back on the rock to stare at the water as it washed up toward me. The sounds of chatter and people laughing enveloped me as I began sifting through my phone looking for something relaxing to listen to. It didn't take long before I was peacefully asleep with the soulful sounds of my favorite band playing softly behind the clashing of the ocean waves.

"Esteban! She ripped the screen again, she's gone!" I heard Gloria yell in the distance as I darted onto the busy streets with my pack tightly strapped around me. Running, I didn't look back. With quivering lips and skin as cold as stone, I wasn't sure if I would make it through the night most times, but I refused to go back. I found myself alone in this big world of people, millions of people, just trying to make it through the next day, staying as far away from Esteban as I could. I spent months on the streets, surviving with the skills I had learned from Piper, or bouncing between friends until I was picked up by the authorities and brought back to Esteban for being a runaway.

Repeating the process all over again, I would wait for my escape and then venture off into the world again, until finally I was trapped under his roof with an ankle monitor and forced to stay locked inside the house with them. I tried my best to listen to them, tell them everything they wanted to hear, and mimic their daughter's actions until Esteban began touching me again.

I went to school with a baseball-sized bruise on my leg from attempting to fight back. He was much stronger than I was, and no matter how hard I fought, he always had the advantage. I think he enjoyed watching me kick and scream. Laughing he would squeeze my arms and mock me while he pinned me down.

After so many failed attempts at running away, trying to play nice, asking people for help, and trying to convince the officers not to take me back to him, it didn't matter. He had already painted the picture that I was a rebellious teen who had spent too much time on my own. "She needs discipline, I can't control her." He told social workers and the court that I refused to follow directions and he began fearing for his own safety because of how destructive I was.

The longer we spent in and out of courthouses and lost in a system that never listened to a word I said, the more frustrated I became. I wanted someone to see me, to *hear* me. But Esteban took all of the fight I had and showed me that I was weak. There was nothing I could do to hurt him with my feeble attempts to defend myself, so after a time, I knew that fighting was useless. I needed to try something else instead. When I was sure he was coming after me again, I slid into the bathroom and grabbed a bottle of his painkillers out of the cabinet.

As I wrapped my lips around the faucet, I began chugging water and tossing pills into the back of my throat like candy. I was so angry that the entire bottle disappeared within a matter of seconds. *Oh well.* As I sat on the floor cradling my legs near my chest, I began to feel sharp pains in my stomach, and for 15 minutes I sat there clenching an empty bottle in my hand waiting for him to beckon me out of the bathroom.

At this point I had lost everything that mattered to me, my dignity, my siblings, my friends, school, and basically everything I cared about. I had grown tired of running, hiding, and pretending to play nice with his family. My body felt light, and everything was foggy. His voice sounded like it was far away as he reached down and whispered into my ear, "gringa bitch." I could feel the inner depths of my soul shattering while I lay there lifeless without fight. Empty inside, I fixated my eyes on a tiny little crack in the ceiling while he continued to tear at my body. The sharp pains in my stomach continued to worsen, and I knew I might overdose but I didn't care. Laughing to himself, he grabbed my throat and held me down, "Te gusta?"

Laughing manically, I sluggishly held my hand up in front of his face and opened my fist, revealing the empty yellow bottle of his medication.

"Oh dios mio."

As I lay there laughing in pain, Esteban disappeared and everything else became a blurred haze of strange voices and bright lights, and the next thing I knew someone was shoving plastic tubes into the back of my throat. I could feel the pressure of the tube against my esophagus as vague shapes of people moved around me in all directions. *Am I dying, wait, I didn't actually want to die.* I tried to speak but no words were coming out, and the thick tube sitting in my throat made it difficult to breathe. An unfamiliar pungent acidic flavor lingered in my mouth, causing me gag continuously.

"It's okay sweetie," the nurse beside me said, placing her hand in mine and squeezing it tightly while another ripped the tube out of my mouth. Her voice was gentle and soft, making it easy to close my eyes and rest.

—

I awoke sometime later in another unfamiliar bed, wearing a hospital gown and a bandage where an IV would have been. I wandered out of the hospital room and was greeted by a nurse.

"Well good morning, How do you feel?"

"I do-I don't know…"

"Well, let's just go have a seat on your bed for a minute," she said sternly.

As she walked me toward my bed, I realized that this room was unlike any hospital I had ever seen. It resembled a hospital room, but there was something different about it. The walls were bare, and the room was empty except for two beds that lay adjacent to one another, with a small sofa in the corner of the room. The windows didn't open, and the bathroom near the entrance to the room had no door.

"Welcome to Heritage Oaks, You're going to be staying with us for a while so that we can assess you and figure out what's going on, okay?"

It took a few moments before I realized that I was a patient in a mental hospital for children. I couldn't remember much about the night before, but I knew that, like the children's hospital, I was safe here.

The following weeks were spent talking to other children my age, creating sketch drawings, and choking down handfuls of medication, Zoloft they called it. The staff members insisted that I was depressed and that I needed to take it, so I could feel better. *I'm not depressed, you imbeciles.* But the self-inflicted scars on my body said otherwise, so I took the emotion-suppressing medicine anyway. When I was released back to Esteban, I had forgotten what made me so angry in the first place. But after a while, I had begun to recognize the effect it was having on me and I didn't like it. I couldn't focus in class, and I could easily doze off while standing. I felt like a walking zombie. I knew that the medication had changed me, so I decided to stop taking it without telling anyone. It wasn't long before my old self came back.

I wanted to leave, I wanted to talk to my siblings, I wanted to visit my grandmother, and I wanted to go back to my mother's house regardless of what she had done in the past. I knew that at least there I would be free. When the social workers explained to me that she had lost her parental rights and there was no chance that I would be going back to her, I was devastated. I didn't miss her, but I wanted to be anywhere other than back with my father. But once again, no one listened to me.

Esteban hadn't touched me since the incident with the bottle. I knew it scared him and I was proud of that. Finally, I was no longer afraid him or maybe I just didn't give a fuck anymore.

We had one last altercation before I was arrested and placed in juvenile hall. I had been coming home late from school for weeks and refused to obey anyone. I started smoking weed with friends, drinking in abandoned houses and camping at the river, chatting about everything under the moon. I was officially wild.

One night, when I came home, Esteban was waiting to lay into me. Gloria, his wife, urged Giselle into the other room while as Esteban began slamming me against the wall yelling a slew of profanities.

"You're not allowed to do whatever the hell you please"

It was pointless to give him an explanation. Refusing to acknowledge his questions infuriated him even more and I enjoyed that.

"Where have you been this whole time!?"

"None of your business."

"You're going to be just like your mother. Do you want to be like her?"

As I pushed him away from me, my hand found its way to his face. I slapped him with all of my strength and began dodging the incoming fist's he threw at me. For a moment I was possessed with aggression, I felt powerful.

"Touch me again, and I'll kick your ass," I hissed.

He was so surprised that he let me walk away and into the bedroom, where I locked the door and cried myself to sleep on the floor.

"America, wake up." an unfamiliar voice said.

I opened my eyes and saw two officers standing in my room holding handcuffs. I'd been arrested before for running away from Esteban, but this time was different. One of the officers told me I was going to the juvenile hall, said I would stay there until I could straighten my act up.

"Good, I *hope* I stay there. You should have come a long time ago" I said sarcastically.

"Do you understand what juvenile hall is like? It's not a fun place to be. You're not going on vacation."

"Yeah, I got that, but I'm sure it's better than this fucking house, so let's go. What are you waiting for? Start the car," I snapped.

The ride to juvie was quiet. The two men said very little until I broke the silence with questions that seemed to take them off guard. "Can I stay here until I'm eighteen?" They looked at each other in confusion, so I repeated myself.

"No, this isn't a long-term facility. It doesn't work like that."

"Then how long can I stay here?"

"That depends on if your dad presses charges and how long your sentence is. Who knows, could be a while."

"Good," I replied.

As I entered the facility, different intake officers made me remove my clothing and told me to bend over, squat, and cough.

They said that they had to make sure I hadn't brought any surprises along with me. Naked and vulnerable, I did as they said. They let me shower and gave me a set of inmate clothing, the fabric was rough, and the pants were itchy. Nothing fit the way it was supposed to. The shoes were made of a blue, canvas like cloth, and the rubber soles squeaked with every step that I took. With my hands interlaced and tucked into my waist line, I stepped in front of a camera to take my picture for the new plastic wristband they were going to slap on me.

Smiling, they snapped a photo of my face and told me that the plastic bracelet was to be worn at all times, and that if I removed it at any point there would be repercussions. The thick chunky bracelet was made of clear plastic and pinned together with a metal hook that fit tightly around my wrist, encased within the plastic was the photo I had just taken along with a few different reference numbers, and my birth date. I felt like I had officially lost my identity and become a number in their system.

I spent a few months in juvenile hall, hours on ends were spent just sitting in a cell, trying to learn to read the bible because that's what other kids were doing, and it was one of the few books they allowed us to keep. I was terrible at reading and attempting to understand what seemed like a whole new language frustrated me. I flipped the pages, it all seemed so pointless, but I had nothing better to do anyway except look at pictures. The cell consisted of four blue concrete walls, a thin makeshift mattress on a metal frame and toilet in the center. The doors were heavy and thick and had a little window near the top which allowed the officers to check on us every so often.

Laying on my bed with my butt against the wall and my feet folded above me, I would lay there trying to read while looking at pictures upside down, trying to bring each story to life with my eyes. It was difficult to understand, I was unfamiliar with most phrases and words, and a lot of it seemed to tie into nothing, where one story would end another would just begin, and the scriptures and lines were so confusing, sometimes I couldn't tell if I was reading the same story. I would sit for hours each day, sometimes reading what little I could, sometimes doing nothing at all. Time fell away, and each day became a blur. That dull routine became a part of me. Wake up, line up for breakfast, eat, exercise to some old workout video that Paula Abdul created in the 90's, then shower, try to read, eat, exercise, and sleep. Rinse, wash and repeat. I had missed my friends, my school and the world beyond these walls, but I wasn't ready to leave just yet.

I knew that I didn't deserve to be there, but it sure beat sleeping on the cold hard streets or at Esteban's house. Still, I could feel my brain shriveling as each day passed. I wondered how we were supposed to learn and grow and become independent if we spent more than half of our days sitting in a cell. *The hall is bullshit.*

When it came to showering, girls went in groups to take quick 10-minute showers before trading places with the next group. A tall metal pole stood in the middle of the room, surrounded by several shower heads spitting out hot water in all directions. The tiles were cold beneath my feet as I stumbled across the slippery floor, and to the center of the room where the shower pole stood. Naked and bare, I was exposed under the steaming hot water. One tall rectangular window was set in the wall closest to the entrance, and behind it, an officer glancing in every so often.

"Come on ladies, hurry it up!" A voice shouted form the other side of the window.

"Quickly! We're on a timed schedule, quickly ladies, let's go!" every day was the same.

The shower felt good as I dipped my head beneath the hot water, letting drips run down my face and slide down my back. Eventually, I started to feel safe in that stone facility and looked forward to the cinnamon buns they served us on Sunday mornings. No one could hurt me there, and for once, I was actually able to rest.

As I started becoming comfortable, my probation officer met with me to break the news I would be going home soon. Time flew by quickly in juvenile hall and I had thoroughly impressed everyone while I was there. I was focused, I listened, and I didn't talk back. After a while, a part of me began to enjoy the simple routine that I first despised. It was nice, and I easily maintained my "honors" status which allowed me a few extra inmate perks, things like candy, longer showers and movie time on Friday's. Just as I started to settle in – *bitch wants me to leave?*

"I don't fucking get it! I've told you over and *over* again, I don't want to go there!"

"Well look, right now that is the only option okay? Now unless there is another *reason* you want to give me, as to why I shouldn't send you back, that's where you're going, O.K.?"

I couldn't tell my probation officer the truth- *Esteban would just make me seem like a liar anyways.*

"No, it's not O.K." I said.

I spent the days prior to my release doing everything I could possibly imagine to make them angry, but nothing worked. I was going back "home."

"See you in a few days when I run away again," I half-joked to the officer that gave me my belongings before sending me to the very last place on earth that I wanted to be. Once there, I took the first chance I had to leave. Within days I turned myself into the station as a runaway and was placed back in the facility that I was released from, back to D-Unit.

I had run away more times than I could count before someone took me seriously. I was finally assigned a new social worker and child attorney who sat with me in a tiny glass room in the juvenile hall building. As we sat there, she listened to me explain the many reasons why I refused to go back to Esteban's house. *Someone finally listened.*

"So, then you would rather choose foster care? Over going back home?"

"That is *not* my fucking home, and yes. I don't care what that is, but sign me up," I told her.

The short Latina woman sat up straight in her chair and began jotting down notes as we continued to speak. Not long after our conversation, we entered the courtroom where I was finally deemed "a ward of the court" and placed into foster care under Child Protective Services. I felt a weight lift off my shoulders as the judge announced the final decision. After one last investigation and with both parental rights terminated, I was done with that chapter of my life and ready to move onward and into foster care. I didn't know exactly what that meant, but I knew that anything would be better than every place I had been before.

CHAPTER THIRTEEN

The Foster Monster

I awoke a few hours later to find that my bottle of liquor had vanished, and the tide was kissing the tips of my toes. Drowsy, I stood up and took a quick glance around. For a moment I forgot where I was and how I had gotten there. And then the realization of everything hit me like a ton of bricks. I could feel my heart swell like the tide below my feet. I ripped the headphones from my ears and tossed the old iPod in the water. *I won't be needing that.*

I began walking, barefoot and aimless along the shore. I enjoyed the way the tiny pebbles felt between my toes, and with each step I took, I felt the tension in my body dissipate. It was magical the way the ground absorbed the pressure of my foot in an instant. For a moment I began running along the shore, counting the seconds between the time my feet hit the ground until my footprints disappeared with each wave that washed onshore.

As strangers walked past me in the midst of the winter weather, they looked at me in disbelief and stared for longer than they should have. Typically, I would have never danced on the beach for no reason, but today I didn't care. Today, the world was at my feet, and everyone that once mattered to me felt utterly obsolete. It was like standing there, next to a big, beautiful body of water that never seemed to end just made sense. My problems were ash in the wind, Jordan… and her face. They were easy to forget when I looked out into the open water.

"Well this place looks fun," I announced to the social worker as we walked toward the entrance to a big house-like facility.

As I grew older and the foster homes became scarce, It became challenging to find placements with a family that understood me or wasn't using me as a source of income. I wanted so badly for someone to accept me and love me, but I knew that no one would, so I began self-sabotaging placements, knowing I would be moving again anyways. More often than not, every home was just another place to sleep temporarily until the next home was found. After multiple failed placements, I was finally placed in a group home at sixteen. As I entered my late teens, I realized that most youth in foster care that were my age, were becoming too old to find a stable home. I knew most that people wanted babies and young children, not an emotionally troubled teen with nothing but some lousy past, and painful scars to show for it.

It felt so unfair, I didn't deserve that "bad kid" label. *Ya, sure I had a bad mouth and ran away a lot, but I'm not like any of these kids.* I was different, and everyone around me knew it. There was just nothing to be done about it. It was too late.

The group home was infested with neglect, drugs, underage sex and moldy food that sent children to the hospital with food poisoning. It wasn't uncommon for these things to occur in an under-budgeted facility short on staff and supplies. I spent nearly a year hiding in my room until the day Ms. Fiona saved me. I used to spend my free time just lying in bed, watching the light shine through my window and move through my room. Some days went by faster than others, yet they all seemed too similar and perfectly hollow, no matter how often I tried to distract myself with art, but it hardly worked. Just outside my room were other kids my age in the same depressing situation, living the same depressing life. I felt less alone knowing that there were other children without families and kids no one wanted, other troubled teens like myself. But I couldn't escape the feeling that we were all unwanted.

For hours on end, I would stare at the walls that held me captive, concealing me from the outside world. That remarkably dull cerulean blue seemed to color every inch of my day. The floors were cold and hard, and though the beds were stiff, they were soothing. It was the first time in my whole life that I had been in a stable living environment.

I knew that stiff bed was the only thing that wouldn't slip out from beneath me. Every day that bed consoled me. Waiting to encase my little body in solace beneath its sheets. It held me close and kept me warm like no one else ever had. It was comforting knowing that when days were growing weary and cold, I could look forward to melting between those sheets that tightly wove around my body.

At this point in my life everyone I had ever known had given me up. I told myself there must have been something inside me that everyone else saw but I couldn't. I didn't understand why I wasn't deserving of a good family. I would lay on that bed mentally spinning myself in circles. *Was I always going to be this lonely? What's going to happen once I'm 18 and they toss me out on the street? Where do I go?*

Battling with emotions I didn't understand, I was terrified of what the future held. I'd always been independent my whole life, always been strong, always felt as though I could handle anything that came my way because I had no other choice. I wasn't interested in escaping with drugs anymore, I hated sex and I never wanted to do bad things like other kids my age. I wanted more out of life. I wanted the simple things ordinary people took for granted: I wanted a family, a *real* home. I saw people, children and families torn apart because of choices they made, because of a broken system that let them down, because no one cared enough. I never wanted to be that statistic, I never wanted to be that "failure rate" everyone talked about.

As terrible as my time was transitioning through that group home, I made friends in that facility that I'll never forget, people I will always look back on lovingly and hope they turned out ok. But then there were the tormented ones with their own demons driving them to do ferociously nasty things, looking for trouble and an outlet to release their anger. I didn't want to be like some of those other kids dwelling outside my bedroom door. I was over that anger, I was safe. Lonely and depressed, but safe nonetheless.

Some of children that swept through the group home were hateful and cruel, they let their emotions control them, but I could still see that little flicker of a light they held within, even if it was over-shadowed by this plaguing darkness that surrounded us all. I watched children change in that place, they lost themselves and after time, lost that light. I didn't want to be like them. I was going to be different, but I was running thin on patience and could feel a shadow of doubt lingering over my soul. *How will I live? Where will I live when I leave here?* All I ever wanted was someone to love me, but no one ever did, until I met Fiona.

Fiona was our onsite school teacher at the group home, and an excellent one at that. She helped all of us with homework assignments and was very patient with the rowdy outbursts in class. I kept to myself most days, and every so often I would glance up and catch her staring at me, smiling. I didn't understand it at first, why this woman kept looking at me. I hadn't done anything wrong, turned in all of my assignments on time, and was ahead of everyone in class. I was literally doing everything I possibly could, so I didn't know what she wanted from me.

Some days she would keep me behind in class while all the other students left and were guided back toward their bedrooms on the opposite side of the building. I would help her prepare for the next school day and chat with her about simple things that I enjoyed, like drawing and writing. She seemed to enjoy my company and always asked more questions, which I never minded answering because it was nice having someone invested in how I felt.

Fiona and I quickly became friends and not long after I had arrived at the group home, an onsite social worker approached me to ask if I'd enjoyed my time there. *Is this a trick question?*

"Well uh, this place sucks," I told her.

"Aww sweetie, I know." she laughed, patting my hand.

"How would you like to leave and try and another foster home?"

Confused, I waited for her to continue talking but instead, the door behind us opened up, and Mrs. Fiona walked in, dressed very casually like she was ready to go jogging or hiking. The car keys in her hand jingled a bit as she walked toward us and sat down beside the social worker-Allison.

"Hi honey" Fiona exclaimed.

As I listened to Allison explain that Fiona would like to take me home and out of the group home, I felt a little excitement rise from deep within. *Is this seriously happening right now?* I had grown very fond of Fiona over the past few months, and without realizing it, we developed an attachment like I had never experienced. I wasn't sure if I could consider her a friend, a mentor, or just an outstanding teacher, but she inspired me to continue working hard every day in class, and I confided in her when I felt like the group home was sucking the soul right out of my body.

By the end of the conversation, I learned that Fiona had decided to get a foster care license and had been working really hard the past few weeks to get certified. She had approached the staff and asked them if it was possible to foster me, so there we all sat together in a dimly lit room in the back of the facility waiting for me to answer.

"Would you like to come home with me?"

"Yes!" I cried, jumping into her arms.

Allison clasped her hands together and smiled while the group home facilitator stepped in to the office to fill out some paperwork with Fiona. A few days later I had packed my belongings and waited anxiously for Fiona to arrive. All of the friends I had made during my stay there wrote letters of encouragement and wished me luck on my new adventure.

Make sure you win the lottery and come back and save us!

Good luck America, I love you so much! I'm going to miss you! Write me!

I'm so happy for you America! See you on the flip side!

At least one of us is getting out of this hellhole, good luck girl!

CHAPTER FOURTEEN

A New Life

A few miles down the beach from where I started, I stumbled across a sea pigeon that seemed to have trouble moving. He sat very still near the water's edge with his wings tucked in. With every passing wave, he tried to stand and run away from the water that so desperately wanted to pull him under. Once the wave passed, he sat still, trying to catch his breath before the next pull of the tide. I could tell he was injured and I immediately wanted to help him. I must have seen at least twenty people walk right past him without a second glance, and it angered me. They clearly noticed him struggling but refused to help him! *How cruel.*

As I drew closer, I was reminded of the little girl I once was, the little girl I lost in the wreckage of the life that I had lived. I jogged closer to the little bird and sat down beside him, blocking the next incoming wave. I sat within centimeters of this little creature, and he didn't seem to mind at all. He seemed relieved that my body shielded him from the next oncoming wave. I had given him enough time to catch his breath and gain some mobility, but I could tell by the way he was acting that he didn't have long to live. *I'm not going to let him die alone.* "It's okay, I gotcha," I told him softly, reaching out and touching the tip of his beak. He hardly moved. Instead, he closed his eyes and let me caress him. He wasn't like any bird I had ever seen before. He was gray and black with patchy white spots along his wings.

109

His underbelly was entirely white and his beak was long and pointy and nearly the same color as the sand. I instantly fell in love with him and knew that I needed to get him away from the water because I had decided that I was going to save him! I refused to stand by and watch him drown.

"I'll be right back," I told him before dashing off to grab a plastic bag I had seen a few hundred feet back. I wanted to move him, but something inside told me not to touch him with my bare hands again. Kneeling beside the bird, I placed the bag next to him and began talking to him as though he could understand me.

"Look, little guy, you're tired… so, I'm going to help you okay?" I whispered to him.

He closed his eyes, and I imagined that was his way of giving me his blessing to wrap the plastic around his body. When I lifted him from the sand, he didn't resist but instead opened his eyes as if he was curious about where I was taking him. I tried to scope out the best place to let him rest away from the shore, but there were so many people lined up along the sand that it was difficult to decide where to go. As I stood there helplessly holding the bird, an older gentleman in his 40s walked up to me, smiling.

"I watched you," he said.

I looked at him in confusion as I held the bird in front of me. *The fuck?*

"What do you mean?" I asked.

"Well I saw what you did for the bird, and I admire that. Many people walked past him and didn't do a single thing."

"Oh, yeah…" I said, still slightly confused.

"Well anyway, let's find a place we can leave him," he told me.

The tall, dark-haired stranger pointed to a shaded slope about half a mile away, so I tucked the bird under my arm and began following him to the hill away from the shore. I didn't talk much to the strange man who said he had been watching me. My first priority was finding a beautiful place to rest this little bird. Everything else came second.

"Can I call you mom?" I asked her on the car ride to my new house.

"Oh honey, you can call me anything you like," she said holding my hand as we drove away from the group home and onto the busy streets of the city.

The following year and a half I spent with Fiona was one of the best years I had ever experienced. I was a child for the first time in a long time. We went on camping trips, every so often had a girl's night where we shopped and had dinner together. We watched movies at the theater and talked for hours on end. San Juan High School was the first school I was able to stay at for more than a year since elementary school. I even attended my first dance with Fiona as my date.

Life with Fiona was unlike anything I had ever known. She took care of me in all the ways a mother should and showed me what it meant to live carefree. I excelled in all studies and had the freedom to express myself and dress however I pleased, even if that meant fishnet stockings, torn shirts with studded belts, and crazy hairstyles. She continued to love me for who I was, and I wasn't afraid to be myself around her. I didn't have to worry about anything, I trusted her.

My junior year in high school was thrilling. I enrolled myself in student government and helped produce the school yearbook. I took as many extracurricular activities as I could and even starred in the school play, "Night of the Living Dead," inviting my social worker and probation offer to watch me perform alongside my peers. I was able to develop my passions and make "normal" friends, and everything about being there made me feel like a child.

I'll never forget the first crush I had, the first boy that stole my heart and made me feel alive. As Joseph and I would race through the empty fields behind campus and climb through a tiny hole in the fence behind his house, laughing, we would hold hands while making our way through his house.

At sixteen I experienced the innocence of what it felt like to enjoy a real kiss. Not my first kiss. My first *real* kiss. We sat on his bed wrapped in each other's arms. It was sweet, and like nothing I had encountered before, but it scared me a little, so I spent the next few weeks at school pushing him away because it was easier to pretend like I didn't care instead of letting someone get close. I had a difficult time letting people close.

Fiona was the first person in a long time that I let in and she gave me the opportunity to experience so many things I had never done before. My junior year in high school was about developing a sense of who I was. It was about making mistakes, finding out what my passions were, making memories. High school was about the connections I had with friends, the kind of friends that met up before and after school every day because we couldn't get enough of each other. It was about understanding what it meant to feel something other than all this pain I had experienced for so many years, and I lived for every moment with her until it ended. My junior year in high school was about finding out what it meant to be loved, in more than one way.

Above all, my junior year was about the freedom I experienced while living with Fiona. She encouraged me to enjoy my passions while believing in me and trusting me like no one else ever had.

"I'll pick you up in a little while," she would tell me as she dropped me off at the local ice rink. I would take a deep breath and the brisk air would caress my lungs with a frosty warmth. I loved it. Gliding onto the ice was always so easy. My legs naturally began to take control and then I would begin spinning into oblivion. No thoughts, just movement.

The countless hours Piper and I had spent watching people dance made it that much easier to navigate the cold hard ice beneath me. After enough time in that rink, and with the help of friends I had made, I became one of the little ice dancers Piper and I used to envy from the bleachers at Iceland. The faster I would spin, the easier it was to forget the world around me, to forget everyone I had loved and lost. My hands moved in sync with the rest of my body as I stretched them above my head in an attempt to touch the sky.

I felt like a ballerina, as the thin blade under my feet etched circles into the ice. It took months before I could perfect a flawless turn, but every pain was worth the effort. Figure skating gave me a sense of security and control over my life. I was the one who made the decision to spin, or dance, or race in never ending circles, no one could stop me. No one could catch me. My life had been a constant never- ending circle of pain, but these circles were delicate and beautiful.

I never felt an ounce of exhaustion during my session, only pure joy and an overwhelming thirst for more. It wasn't until the whistle blew and the children were ushered off the ice that fatigue would suddenly overwhelm me, and then I'd remember that I needed to catch my breath and look for Fiona.

"Did you have fun honey?" she would say each time.

"Yeah mom, it was great!"

Sitting in the bleachers above the rink, I would unravel my long laces and watch as a big powerful blue machine swept away the remnants of what I had done just moments before. That machine scored ice and left a glossy fresh canvas. I wanted to live in that rink. I wanted to live with Fiona forever. I finally felt at *home*.

CHAPTER FIFTEEN

Goodbye Again

It was easy to forget why I had driven to the ocean to begin with, especially when all of my attention was focused on saving Milo's life. That's what I called him anyway, "Milo." I wanted him to die with a name because it just seemed wrong leaving him nameless and cold to drown in the ocean.

I settled Milo down into the slope of the sand dune and sat beside him staring at the ocean beyond us. The stranger sat beside me and began to question me,

"Why, " he said, "Why did you do that?"

The question lingered in the air momentarily before I dared to answer as the short Hispanic man sat there beside me, waiting patiently for an answer. The truth was simple and easy to explain, but for some reason, the words wouldn't come out.

Had I been that bird, would anyone have stopped to help me? Had anyone ever stopped to help me, growing up the way I did? And the answer was no. The people I was supposed to trust, were the ones that hurt me the most, and so many others saw my suffering, but did so little to help me.

For a moment I could relate to Milo, I could feel his pain and understand what it must have felt like to sit in an enormously populated area, drowning while strangers glanced your way and continued their busy day without a second thought. It wasn't right. It angered me. I wanted someone to help Milo like I wanted someone to help me. And then it hit me: I just wanted help. Then, now, and every day in between, I just wanted someone to be there for me as a child when no one else was. I wasn't going to leave Milo alone, not today.

"I watched many people walk past that bird, and you were the only person to stop. So, tell me huh? *Why* did you help him?"

"Because I loved how much strength and will to *live* he had"

My explanation to the dark-haired stranger seemed much too long and detailed once I finally found the words to say, rattling off my entire life story and meaningless existence, sobbing between sentences. But oddly enough, he listened patiently to the whole story. Picking up a handful of dirt and letting it sift through his thick fingers, the stranger took a deep breath before letting out a long sigh.

I turned over to look at him, puzzled and half expecting him to just get up and walk away, but he didn't. He just kept picking up handfuls of sand and squeezing it between his fingers as though he were frustrated.

"Look, I understand... I do..." he said.

"What do you mean?" I asked him.

"Why do you think you ended up here? Sitting here right now with me..."

"Because I-I-I wanted to save that stupid bird and you were stalking me," I jokingly huffed between sobs.

"No, it's because you were meant to be here, right now, at this very moment," he said.

I continued to sob with my hands covering my face while the man without a name began to ramble on about life and its purpose. He explained to me that not everything happens the way we imagined it would. He told me that we are meant to learn from our past, to evolve into better people, stronger people. But I didn't feel so strong.

"And that gives us purpose, knowing that we can take our experiences and grow from them. That's what gives this life meaning, what gives *us* meaning," he continued on.

"Had you been like anyone else on that beach, you would have just walked away from Milo. Now he has another chance to live, whatever it is inside you that makes you different, is beautiful."

Maybe he was right, this complete stranger, I had never heard it put quite like that. As I began to ponder my existence, listening to him ramble on, my eyes were drawn to the open water before me. We watched the waves dance together, protecting the little bird as we continued to share experiences and enjoy each other's company. His words resonated with me. Lost in the sea, I felt my energy change as I stared into the distance at the water's now profound blue brilliance, shimmering in the distance.

"Honey, you can't tell your social worker. Don't mention him on your next visit ok? He's just going to be here for a little while." Fiona said in confidence.

"Why… can't I say anything?"

"Well, because he's not technically supposed to be here, but he's your brother, so it's fine," she whispered as if someone were listening.

It wasn't long before the rug was pulled from beneath my feet again. As much as I had loved my new mom, I watched our relationship begin to falter after about a year and a half, when her son moved in - my new brother. I knew early on that things were going to change, I just didn't know how much. Her middle son was a raging alcoholic and reminded me of the way Dana would act after a few drinks. When he was sober, it was easy to tolerate him, but once the liquor set in, everyone in sight needed to run for the hills. Fiona loved him and let him do just about anything he wanted as long as it made him happy, all the while enabling him to drink in the house.

I kept her little secret, I didn't tell my social worker the next time she asked about how I was doing. I was afraid of losing Fiona, so I didn't say anything about the broken dishes and angry outbursts Edgar had. I didn't tell her about the time he locked me outside for hours because I didn't give him a beer quickly enough, or how he punched holes in my bedroom door. "URrrr justaaa little cunt, shesh mine mom you bisssshhh!" he screamed, kicking me on the floor and begging me to fight with him. I didn't. Instead, I cried myself to sleep waiting for Fiona to come into my room and console me, but she never did. Most times I would slip out of the bedroom window and leave drunken Edgar in a pile of his own vomit. *Fiona can clean that up.*

I stopped trusting my new mom and began calling her by her first name again. I started staying at school late or spent as much time with friends as I could, for as long as possible - until I was forced to leave. After a few weeks with him in the house, I decided to pack my bags and leave.

One night, A light from down the hall beamed into my bedroom and woke me. I fumbled down the hallway and toward the light, ready to switch it off, but a noise caught me off guard. Peering around the corner and into the living room, Fiona was sitting with her legs propped on the couch, a glass of wine in her hands. I always enjoyed pouring Fiona's alcohol and taking a few sips from the cup before handing it to her, and she liked teaching me the difference between fine wine and that "cheap rubbish stuff." Edgar was sitting next to her. "You have to stop," she whispered softly to him.

"Mom, it's not fair, I'm your son! I need help! I can't go back there."

"But you're not even supposed to be here for that long, you know that I can get in real trouble with the county because of her."

"Mom you work for the county! Just figure something out, please. I'm your blood."

"I know, baby," she said.

Your blood? Because of her? I repeated the statements in my head. Fiona had told me countless times, "Just because you share the same blood with someone else, that doesn't make you family. God put you in someone else's body, but you're *my* daughter." *That was a lie.*

I didn't need to hear anything else. I could tell she had already made up her mind up. She was going to get rid of me. *Dana, Fiona, fuck you both.* I had seen this too many times before. She wanted to get rid of me. As I quietly made my way back toward my bedroom, I decided to start packing clothes, a few journals, my favorite things, and stuff I might need before the foster monster could send me on my way. I just needed to say goodbye to my friends at school. *I never get to say goodbye.* I decided against leaving right then and put off my escape until tomorrow. My bedroom door hung open, the hinges busted and broken. I tucked my bag under my bed and went to sleep listening to soft whispers lingering in the hall.

CHAPTER SIXTEEN

Strangers Everywhere

It had been awhile since we first met. The sun had barely begun to warm up the early afternoon sky, the alcohol had slowly begun losing its effect, my tears had run dry. Somewhere during the conversations, we exchanged phone numbers.

"You remind me of my daughter, Should you ever need anything, give me a call."

"Mhm." I nodded.

It had only taken an hour for him to show me that there was more than a quivering weakness in my bones. There was a light that I didn't know still existed, and Milo was proof as he sat there contently chirping beside me. I could tell the rest had given him a bit more energy than he had before. Tilting his head around, he looked in all directions. I was slightly shocked that he was still sitting there next to me, but he seemed so content and happy that another part of me was inspired by his enthusiasm. In one way or another, I suppose we all struggle, and yet somehow, he dared to happily chirp through it all.

I wanted to explore San Francisco just a little while longer before I went to the golden gate bridge, my final stop. I hadn't done much since the day began, but I already felt better than I had before.

I had felt a sense of relief wash over me as I spilled my most private thoughts out loud to a stranger. Looking around, not much had changed except the color of the sky which had gone from an alluring golden color to a vibrant bright blue as the fog gently blew away. It was difficult to see where the sky met the ocean. I rubbed my finger across Milo's beak and walked away, knowing that he'd be okay. "Bye little guy."

With each step forward, I became lost in the beauty that surrounded me. That stranger had left me battling with what he called, "A different perspective."

Maybe I have been looking at everything all wrong. For the first time in a long time, I had let someone in and he passed no judgments, instead gave me advice and words of encouragement. It was the most helpful thing anyone had done for me in a long time, and it was exactly what I needed without realizing it. Jordan and I hadn't spoken like this in years. My relationship with him had been broken for quite some time, and frankly, neither of us knew how to fix it

"Can you just write your number down here, I promise I'll call you when I can."

The next day at school I began collecting phone numbers from everyone that I possibly could. I had planned on running away after school, but I didn't tell anyone. Right before the bell rang, I was called up to the front office where Fiona waited for me. She told me that we were going to grab some ice cream and chat a little bit. *Sure, I can do ice cream... but as soon as we get home, I'm gone.*

We never made it back to the house. Instead, we went out for a quick cone, and Fiona then drove me straight to the office where my probation office sat behind a large table in the middle of a conference room. In my heart, I knew why we were there, and instead of fighting it, I sat next to her and looked at her, defeated.

"What," I said.

"Well, America, Fiona says that you have been having a difficult time lately. She said that you're not behaving, sneaking out of the house, and disappearing for hours."

"So, what?"

"Well, at this point, we aren't willing to give you any more chances, America. You just keep making the same mistakes. What happened? I thought everything was going well? You've been there for almost a year and *a half...*" she seemed desperate for an explanation.

As silence filled the room, I glanced at the door, thinking about whether or not it would be a good idea to just run right out and never look back. "This is such bullshit!" I screamed. *I promised Fiona I wouldn't say anything about Edgar, but how could I keep that promise when she had don't this to me?* I didn't owe her anything now.

"Alright, officer: Kate, my P.O called loudly. "America we are taking you back to juvenile hall. This kind of behavior is just unacceptable."

Suddenly another officer stepped into the room and began walking toward me with handcuffs.

"No no no! Wait!... *hold on...* what do you mean *my* behavior is not acceptable? What about *her* behavior?!" I yelled angrily, pointing to the waiting room where Fiona sat outside.

Both Kate and the officers took one glance at each other and nodded as if to say "continue," so I told them everything that had been going on while under Fiona's care. I told Kate about the drinking, the violence, and the holes in my wall. I cried and explained to her that I only wanted to stay at school longer, so I could swim and dance and join activities like other kids. It was never a problem before Edgar came. Sobbing, I told her how Fiona had betrayed me and how I knew she didn't want me anymore. "I'm just another walking dollar sign!"

"Alright, alright. It's okay" Kate said, wrapping her arms around me. You're not in trouble, it's okay. America, you should have told me sooner."

"Why, so you could take me away again?"

Kate let out a big sigh, "You know that you can't stay there anymore, right? Understand? Her eyes bore down on me.

"Yeah,"

Later that day, I found myself in the same group home that Fiona plucked me out of nearly a year and a half prior. Some of the faces had changed, but for the most party everything remained the same. Upon entering the facility, a staff member handed me a fresh white linen shirt and baggy blue pants and said, "You know the drill girl, get on with your bad self."

Yeah, yeah yeah. I kept telling myself that I would be eighteen in just a few months and that none of this mattered. Soon I could make my own decisions. *Fuck these people.* Grabbing my clothes, I walked to the nearest restroom and removed my "civilian wear" before being officially welcomed back. *I'm almost eighteen, I'm nearly eighteen. I'm going to be eighteen soon. It's okay, America. You got this.*

"Boy / Girl interaction is not allowed.

Food trading/giving away is not allowed

Do not talk in the hallway.

Do not look in windows, even your own.

Do not ask for food (food is a privilege, not a right).

Face the wall while sleeping.

Boys are not allowed to have rubber bands.

Do not drink water from the fountain."

CHAPTER SEVENTEEN

Growing Up

Well *Shit.* I wished I hadn't thrown my iPod into the water. *My brother gave me that iPod.* As I walked further from the bird and along the shore, I found myself repeating the stranger's wise words, "It's all about perspective." *Maybe I've been looking at this all wrong.* As I reflected on my relationship with Jordan, I saw it happen all over again.

As he had come closer for one final goodbye, I held my breath, attempting to stand my ground and show no emotion. "I'll always love you, America." he said, placing his lips on mine one last time. There was a piece of me that wanted him to kiss me, a part of me that hoped he would stay and promise me he would change and that things would be different for us both. But that little girl who fell in love with him years ago needed to let him go. There was too much damage for either of us to ever be okay, and we both knew it.

We were bound by the love we once had for one another and the family we had created, but things were different now. I wasn't the same person he fell in love with, and he wasn't the same boy who whisked me off the streets as a child. Somewhere between emancipation and adulthood, I became an angry, depressed person, and we stopped caring about each other.

I thought leaving the system behind would give me some sort of hope, a sense of peace knowing that no one else controlled my life. I had the power to make decisions that could ultimately make me happy. But instead, within five years, I ended up here awaiting my death. Awaiting the moment when I finally had the courage to jump from the Golden Gate Bridge.

"Damn girl, you're killing it!" A staff member announced. The next few months, I worked hard to maintain my level in the group home. Since I was considered a long-term resident, I had extra privileges as long as I held onto my level. *Guess it's kinda like juvi.* Things like wearing my own clothes, having a private room, going to the movies, and eating whatever I wanted were essential to me, so I made sure to stay on good terms with everyone there, no matter how hard it was at times.

My onsite social worker Paige was a huge help. She told me that I would be there until I emancipated and made sure to reiterate the fact that I needed to learn how to get a job and save money, because once I was eighteen, that was it. I was going to be an independent adult. "K baby doll, we are going to look for a job today," Paige said as we jumped into the company van. We drove all around the city, only stopping to collect applications, fill out paperwork, and hand in resumes. Paige was one of my favorite social workers. She had a contagious laugh that even on your worst day, would make you smile. Even more importantly, she believed in me. As we circled the mall, Paige popped in a CD "Third Eye Blind," she said. "They're so good! I'll play you some of their songs when you come back with that job, baby doll!"

"Yea yea," I said, darting away from the van and into the mall. Wandering the mall aimlessly, I found that most stores were either closed or in the midst of closing, no one gave me the time of day. Losing faith in my ability to successfully turn in applications, or get a job, I started becoming agitated. Eventually, I walked past a red-haired lady who smiled at me through the window from inside a little café. *That was my opening.* I walked up to the window and tugged on the door, it was locked. "We are closed" the woman mouthed from inside the café.

"I need a job!" I yelled at her. She shook her head in disbelief and attempted to walk away from the window, around the corner and out of sight. I stood there waiting. When the red-haired woman reappeared, I said it again, this time knocking on the door. " I need a job!"

"What's up kid? We are closed," she announced as she unlocked the door to talk to me.

"Well, I need a job. My social worker is in the van over there and said we can't go home until I have a job- I'm tired and I want to go back home-here's my resume-I can do anything you need me to- I can start right now-help you close-or anytime you need-just get me out of the group home for a few hours-you don't understand-I need a job. Are you hiring?

"Whoa, Whoa! Whoa! Slow down kid,"

"Can you give me a job or what?" I asked her.

"Sure! Come back tomorrow, What's your name?"

"*What?* Uh, it's A-A-America," I blinked at her.

"Alright, see you tomorrow America." She said as she closed the door on me and smiled again. *What the fuck? That worked? I need to tell Paige.* A few minutes later I came running back shouting at the top of my lungs,

"I did it! I did it! I got a job!"

"No way!" she exclaimed.

"I literally just walked up there… and said, Lady, I need a job. My group home is going to kick me out if I don't find a job, something about being sick of driving around looking…and then she said, ok."

"Wait, you told her what?" Paige said, shocked.

"I just told her I needed a job and she said I could start tomorrow."

Paige laughed hysterically as we drove away listening to her favorite band. *What's so funny?*

Landing my first job was a huge accomplishment at the group home. There were only a few of us that maintained employment throughout our time there. Paige collected my checks and saved every penny for me until the day I left.

On the day of my release, the day I was finally no longer a ward of the court, I told myself things were going to be different. I was going to make something of myself, and nothing was going to hold me back. I held onto the few things I owned: A shirt, a few books, a light sweater. With each step into the vast world before me, I could feel my heart racing faster than it ever had before. This was freedom. *This was my new life.* My hands began to tense, and I thought to myself-*this is it.* The sun fell upon my skin slowly, and then all at once. A warm wind caressed my body. And the atmosphere around me seemed to change suddenly. Everything became clear. I was free, *and alone.*

CHAPTER EIGHTEEN

To the Moon and Back

It didn't matter that I had rolled my pants up, my legs were entirely soaked. The last thing I wanted was to be uncomfortable, but it was too late for that. For miles I walked the shore, kicking my legs as hard as I could at the water that covered my feet and ankles. "I thought there was a cave up this way?" That's what the nameless stranger told me.

As I approached the end of the beach, I looked at the towering cliff that stood before me. Atop the cliff there stood a building made of glass walls and some sort of sign that I couldn't quite make out. To the left of me stood the ocean, and not too far into the water, a massive formation of rocks emerged from the depths of the seafloor.

Birds gathered around the large rocks, flapping and calling out to one another. Slowly, I walked deeper into the water, this time letting the bottom half of my pants become entirely engulfed by the cold, wet sea. As I slid my hands gently across the top of the frigid water, I smiled. Walking further out into the water, I noticed that around the side of the cliff there was a small path. If I ran across quickly enough when the water receded, I could make it out the other side. Tossing my sandals back onto my feet, I trudged forward.

With my body halfway submerged, the ocean tossed me around fiercely. "AHHHHH!! " I screamed as my legs collapsed and my body fell beneath the surface of the water. Bubbling a slew of profanities from beneath the waves I grabbed my foot and held it tightly. Something below the water had punctured my sandal and stabbed straight into my foot. As I flopped around in the water that tried to pull me deeper into the ocean, I kicked off the second sandal and began swimming toward the shore. I made my way toward the other side of the cliff and emerged stumbling onto the sandy beach. The bottom of my foot was smooth and unharmed. *No blood? That hurt like a son of a-Wow! What is that?*

Laughter filled the air around me as I made my way toward another massive rock formation that stood on the shore. It was half engulfed by the water yet easily accessible by the beach. People. People everywhere. Children were playing in the water with their parents and sandcastles were being made right before my eyes. To my right stood rows of old rubble laying atop thick concrete slabs of stone near the foundation of what was once a building.

The wreckage of the building stood between two tremendous cliffs that faced the water. The atmosphere around me suddenly changed as I glanced around to take in all of the people exploring the ruins that surrounded me. I carefully climbed up to the top of the platform and walked along a narrow stone path which lead me to a cave beneath the further cliff. The bones of the ruined building were scattered about the entire shore. Encased within the frame of the thin slabs of concrete, lay a little pond of water with great lily pads and grass-like stems floating about. Walking to toward the bottom of the second cliff, I could see an entrance to a cave. *This must be it.*

Tourists with cameras gathered near the entrance, and as some entered, others left and made their way toward an enormous wooden staircase that stretched for about a mile toward the top of the hill. Taking a deep breath, I followed a group of people into the cave barefoot, entirely soaked, and ready to explore the depths of this dark hole.

I didn't expect the cave to be so magical. As I walked through the entrance, rocks beneath my feet sounded like a thousand crackling eggs shells. Deeper into the cave, about halfway through, there was a big gaping hole right in the middle of the path that was fenced off with metal poles. Leaning over the poles, I could see the ocean below as waves pulled the tide in and out, slamming it against the rocks and splashing my face with water.

I was in a cave in the middle of a city I had never explored. Diving into the remnants of an ancient building. *What happened here? Where did the building go? How did this cave get here?* At the other end of the cave there was a light, so I followed it to a steep drop off that was enclosed by a fence to keep people from plunging into the water. If I squinted, I could see what looked like a lighthouse in the middle of the water. *Cool.*

Curious, I wanted to see if I could get a better look, so I decided to walk back through the shallow cave, out, and up a dirt path to a platform made of stone, giving me a perfect view of the ocean. I must have stood there staring at the open water for at least an hour, lost in thought, lost in the memory of Kaycee.

"You're stuck with us, baby girl," Jordan and I used to tell our niece after smothering her with kisses. She was going to be with us forever, or so we thought. She trusted me, trusted us. I saw her world fall apart the day we told her what was really going to happen. I could tell she didn't understand.

The words slowly fell out of my mouth as Jordan, her social worker and I sat at a little round table in the kitchen.

"You're going to have a new mommy and daddy for a while, but you'll see us again," I tried to say with confidence, in the hopes that it was soothing enough for her to swallow. As my hands found their way to the bottom of the chair, I made sure to grasp tightly, just in case my body betrayed me and I fell over without warning. I saw everything she knew crumble. I saw it, and it broke me. I didn't know if I was going to be able to hold it together for her and make her believe it was going to be okay. I didn't know if it *was* going to be okay.

All I could think about is the way her eyes darted back and forth between Jordan and me, then over to her social worker, Bernadette. She never liked Bernadette, and it had nothing to do with her as a person, because truthfully, Bernadette was just about as good as it gets when it comes to social workers. I knew from experience. She never liked her because she was a social worker, and to Kaycee, that meant Bernadette was going to swipe her away and take her from more people that she loved. *I know the feeling.*

"Swiper, no swiping!" Kaycee exclaimed, whenever Bernadette entered our home, referring to a cute little cartoon she used to watch. It took months before Kaycee could warm up to Bernadette's visits, and just when she finally let her guard down and was able to relax, she lost everything she loved yet again. As we all sat at that little round table, taking turns holding Kaycee while she cried, she asked, "But why, momma?" reaching out to squeeze me with her little pudgy hands. I could tell she was waiting for someone to say that this was all just a big joke, but it wasn't. Jordan and I couldn't take care of her any longer.

"It's just the way things are, baby. They are going to take such good care of you for us." I tried to comfort her as she wrapped herself around Jordan and sobbed uncontrollably. We couldn't take care of her anymore, even though we promised her that she was stuck with us. We just couldn't, and in an instant, I could see that she was a younger version of myself. This beautiful little person who depended on us for her entire existence locked eyes with us, I could feel how shattered she felt. Tear-stained and confused, she kept waiting for us to tell her something different. Searching for a faltering word in our sentences, she watched us, pausing every few seconds to cry some more.

At some point we couldn't take it anymore, Jordan and I broke down weeping with her. *Is this the right thing to do?! How could we do this?* I wanted to tell Bernadette no, that we had changed our minds, that she couldn't take my little girl, but I knew it was too late. There was nothing Jordan, and I could do to salvage the situation. We weren't prepared enough to give Kaycee everything her fragile existence needed. We couldn't help her, I couldn't even help myself.

It took a while, but Bernadette was eventually able to slip Kaycee into the bedroom for a private conversation about her new family, showing her pictures of everyone that she was going to meet, getting her used to the idea without our lingering presence. Meanwhile, Jordan and I just looked at each other in silence at that little table. I was so angry with him, with us, and what had become of my little family.

I dug my nails into that small, round wooden table that held so many memories from both our girls, Lilah and Kaycee. With every scratch, mark, and dent the girls made in that table I had wanted to scream. Now, as we sat there, and I began to really look at each of the marks left behind, wondering what would become of that table. What would become of us? I wasn't sure that I was going to be able to come back from this, but I knew for her sake, I needed to do this, no matter how much I didn't want to.

I had to give her a fighting chance like I never had, and since we couldn't give her that, I needed to entrust these complete strangers to do that for me. I just wanted to know that they loved her as much as I did. I needed to know at least that much.

CHAPTER NINETEEN

In the Middle of the Ocean

The sounds of children screaming as they ran up and down the stairs startled me and I was back in the present moment. Curious about the lighthouse, I decided to walk a path that led into the forest a little bit deeper to see if I could get a better view farther down the coastline. Along the way, I asked people, "Hey, do you guys know what that is out there?" or "Is that a ship? A lighthouse? Can you see it?

Charging through the forest path, I found comfort in the mystery of it all. The fact that I was literally lost with no guidance yet somehow moving each foot forward felt exactly like I'd been there before. Except this time was different. Except for the rumbling sound of the ocean in the background, the forest was much too quiet. A part of me was a bit terrified walking through the dark dirt path, but another part of me, the part that enjoyed it, felt safe concealed within the trees that surrounded me. I entered a clearing and saw a young couple standing near the edge of a lookout, pointing.

"What's over there?" I asked.

"Look! Look! There's a whale right there in the middle of the water! Do you see it?

"No, where?

The thin young woman used the tip of her finger to point directly to a little spot in the middle of the ocean where the creature had been spraying particles of water into the air.

"He's come to the surface for air," she said. "That's what it looks like when they breathe."

As I stood there watching the whales create fountains above the surface, my heart felt suddenly full. *How many creatures live beneath the sea, millions… billions?* I remembered the mermaids mother used to paint on our walls, and for a fraction of a second, I missed her, or at least the idea of her. She must have been so creative in order to paint murals like that. Why had I never thought about it before, how artistic she was? *Such a shame she chose drugs instead.* I could feel myself questioning my emotions. All this time I'd been angry with her, but just then…I felt sort of sad for her. Moments later, another fountain appeared and then a third. "It's a family!" the couple shouted.

I had never seen a whale before, and even though they were in the distance and difficult to spot, I knew they were there, beneath the sea. These living, breathing, beautiful creatures that took everyone by surprise were making their presence known to the world. I thought about Milo momentarily, and suddenly what the stranger said made sense.

Though Milo and these whales were entirely different forms of life, living in near opposite environments, they were both extraordinary! The ability to thrive in their own unique world made them beautiful. *Aren't we all living in our own little worlds?* I'd been so wrapped up in my life, and my emotions, the that I felt… I forgot that there was a bigger world out there. Being submerged in nature had a way of silencing my inner doubting voice and healed my thoughts.

As I continued walking, searching for high ground, I found a staircase that pointed towards the top of a hill, so I followed it. At the top of the stairs, there was a monument and remnants of a ship that was used during some battle decades before I was born. It ready exactly: *"This memorial to rear admiral Daniel Judson*

Callaghan, U.S.N, and his officers, and his men who gave their lives for our country while fighting on board the U.S.S. San Francisco, in the battle of Guadalcanal on the night of 12-13 November 1942, was formed from the bridge of their ship and here mounted on the great circle course to Guadalcanal by the grateful people of San Francisco on 12 November 1950."

As I read the rows of names engraved on the plaque, I suddenly felt overwhelmed with grief for them. Hundreds of men either died or were severely injured, giving their lives to protect ours and everything we held dear. Yet here I was, wallowing in self-pity, ready to give it all away because it was just too much, and I couldn't handle it. Stepping outside of my own mind, I imagined what they must have gone through, and then I realized that the lighthouse I had been seeking was not a lighthouse at all, but perhaps the top of a sunken ship, Maybe even this ship!

"Is that ship out there the U.S.S San Francisco? I asked someone passing by.

" I don't know, I heard there is a whole graveyard of ships near the bridge," an old man said.

As I walked around the memorial, appreciating pieces of what remained from the U.S.S San Francisco, I pressed my hands against the cold shredded steel. I could see where fragments of missiles had blown through the ship. Gently tracing the outline of the metal, I thought about everything those men had lost and compared it to what I had lost over the years. My marriage was over, my niece was gone… my life and everything I had built over the past few years had ceased to exist. But unlike these men, I still had my life and my daughter. Why was I so quick to give that up? That beautiful little girl needed me more than anyone in the world, yet there I was ready to jump off the Golden Gate bridge and give all of that up. What kind of mother would abandon her own child? *Oh, that's right...My mother.*

"It's just for a little while baby, You're going to be with them for a little while ok?" I said.

I'd spent the entire morning preparing Kaycee to go with her new family. It took a few days, but after a while she was excited to "go on an adventure." I don't think she quite understood the fact that she would never see us again. In fact, I knew that she didn't, but I didn't have the heart to tell her that, so I lied to her.

I knew it was wrong and perhaps cruel, but I didn't have it in me to tell her that we would never see her again. If I openly admitted that, I was afraid I would fall apart again, and I couldn't let her see me in pieces. Saying it out loud made it more real. It was happening, and I had to let her go. *Am I really doing this? Can I really say goodbye?* I wanted this to be a good thing for her. Before Jordan and I came along and plucked her out of foster care, a family had been waiting to adopt her, but Child Protective Services gave us priority to foster and take her because we were kin.

I wanted it to be just like any other day, a less traumatizing goodbye I suppose, and it was. I spent the first thirty minutes curling her hair, careful not to burn either myself or her with the iron. It was hard. My hand was shaking the entire time and all I wanted to do was cry and hold her, but I knew she would start asking questions, so I bit my lip hard. *Pull it together, America! Fucking pull it together.*

The water behind my eyes seemed harder and harder to keep at bay. I wiped away tears, careful not to let her see my emotions spiral out of control. My vision was drowning in a salty sea, and with every curl I let fall freely, I took my hand and wiped away a few tears, continuing on.

"Let's put on your dress and Dorothy shoes, baby," I told her. She loved those shoes! Sparkly and red in color, they reminded her of The Wizard of Oz.

"There's no place like home, there's no place like home," she used to giggle as she tapped her heels together while running around the house. Oh, how that noise used to frustrate me! The constant clicking and clacking those shoes made as she ran up and down the halls with those tiny little feet of hers. Funny how little things like that are constantly taken for granted or overlooked. Right then, I wished for nothing more than to hear her giggle and click- clack her way down the hall once more.

With her hair lightly curled in a red and white polka dot dress and sparkly shoes, she looked like a doll. I just wanted to put her on a shelf and let her stay there but as we continued to get ready I had to remind myself that this was going to be a good thing for everyone. She needed this chance at a new life, a life that Jordan and I couldn't give her living so close to his family and everything that ailed her. We pulled into the parking lot and walked Kaycee toward the visitation center where Bernadette waited with the new adoptive family, then we sat outside while she went to see them.

The first time she met them, were the last moments we were going to ever spend with her, and I knew it. "She fell in love with them instantly, and they adore her," Bernadette said as she brought Kaycee back out to us to say goodbye.

Of course, they did! You dumb bitch, I thought to myself angrily. Who couldn't fall in love with my little Kaycee? She had the most amazing eyes! A small smile that melted your heart, and a sweet voice. Her hair never had an exact color to it-there were so many variations of blonde, lighter blonde, brown with a wild spark of golden. It was a color all its own. And her giggle was contagious. When she would smile, she would sometimes stick her tongue between her teeth, a little mannerism I adored.

"Momma they showed me pictures of their house, it's like a big white castle!" she exclaimed. "And when I get there, I get to meet my new sister, the lady and man in there said she's been waiting her whole life for me!" Kaycee laughed with joy. I wasn't ready to let her go, or prepared to give her away, but I had too, I had to be strong for her.

"Really? That's wonderful baby." I said, hugging her and holding her close while every cell in my body shattered. Jordan and Lilah each took their turn squeezing what little pieces of Kaycee they could get their hands on. Afterward she bounced around the waiting room in her beautiful dress, telling us all about her new family. We weren't supposed to see the new family, we only know what Bernadette and Kaycee shared with us, which wasn't much really.

Tearing Lilah away from Kaycee, we said our final goodbye and waved as Bernadette took Kaycee back into the visitation room. Jordan held Lilah, screaming and kicking all the way to the car. She knew Kaycee was leaving for good - we didn't have to tell her. "My purse!" I yelled. I had forgotten my purse inside the building after saying our goodbyes, so I ran back inside with a face full of tears and there they all were. Kaycee, holding hands as they walked out. Smiling, Kaycee said, "Bye momma, I love you,"

"Have fun baby! Be good, ok?" I yelled at her, pausing momentarily to watch them walk away.

"I will, momma" she yelled back, turning and smiling at me.

"Who was that?" the woman whispered to Kaycee loudly as they walked down the street.

"That's my momma," she replied to the lady with yellow hair, turning around one last time to scream,

"I love you!" while shaking the bear I had given her a few months back.

I gave Kaycee my favorite stuffed bear while I was sick in the hospital and Jordan said that she slept with him every night while I was away. When they would come to visit me in the hospital, I would tell her to take care of him until I came home, and she did. I never got that bear back from her, and it was the only thing they let her take when she left. *Goodbye Kaycee.*

CHAPTER TWENTY

A New Perspective

As I explored the structure in depth, I began to feel my perspective change from deep within. I had arrived there today ready to give up, but somehow, through this unintended magical journey, I had fallen in love my past and was falling in love with the city, My soul was lifted, and as I explored this beautiful and unique natural setting, I felt newly awakened.

As I made my way back down the staircase and around the bend of the path, I decided to venture off away from the path that led to the Golden Gate Bridge and explore downhill. A dark mass of trees covered the incredibly steep hill, and with every step I took, I stumbled further down.

The climb downhill was dark and treacherous, but I still enjoyed the adventure as I made my way toward the edge of the cliff. I just wanted to get closer to that ship, and on the way there I encountered a few homeless camps that had been abandoned. In the field beyond the trees, there was an old fire pit and some plastic rimmed chairs that were half folded or broken. I jumped across remnants of clothing and empty bottles. *I could live here like this; I wouldn't mind it one bit.*

Walking toward the edge of the cliff, a small part of me thought about jumping off knowing I wouldn't survive a fall from that height. *Why wait for the Golden Gate Bridge? I could easily die from this shit.* Mostly I thought about everything I had encountered today, and then about my daughter. Looking into the vast ocean, I understood that there was still so much more life to experience, and so many more beautiful places in the world. There is so much I need to show Lilah.

Before the day started, I had told myself that she didn't need me, and that as much as I had loved her, she would be okay without me. But the truth was, she wouldn't. At the time my future had looked utterly bleak and I knew I couldn't be the kind of mother she needed. I thought that I wasn't strong enough for her and kept feeding myself excuses that enabled me to run away, just like I had done my entire life. But maybe I needed to run away this time, and perhaps I also needed to run back. It was like a switch turned on inside me.

In the distance I could see the Golden Gate Bridge. I knew that I was getting closer to the end of the path, but as much as I wanted to continue walking and finish what I set out to do. I also wanted to fight. I found the strength to turn back around and head home to my little girl. I had lost everything that day, but I would have lost so much more had I stayed. With this new-found courage and seemingly new lease on life, I searched for answers within myself. From that moment on I stopped feeling abandoned, confused, and angry, and began searching for answers.

With the sun setting in the distance, I said my final goodbyes to the ocean as if it were an old friend. Making my way back toward the rock I had fallen asleep on that morning, I wept one last time as the water crashed and frothed before me. This journey gave me purpose and showed me how much work I still needed to do. Now, I just needed to use my new-found strength to get through whatever came next, for myself and for my daughter's sake. If she was the only person in the whole world that needed me, then that would be enough for me.

THE END

EPILOGUE

Over the next few months, I contemplated the idea of forgiveness. People always talk about forgiveness and how it sets you free, but how are you supposed to forgive someone who never bothered to care? And when they tried, when my biological mother *thought* she was trying, she only caused more pain.

After a time, I think life just wore her out. The alcohol and drugs overcame her and left us with only memories of who she used to be. We lost her, and she lost her mind. Her delicate beauty slowly faded away and I watched it happen until I couldn't anymore. I gave up on my mother. The abuse and the lifestyle that came along with living beside a jobless alcoholic drug addict. When I gave up on her, I lost my siblings in the process and for the longest time, I blamed myself. I thought maybe I was the cause of everything that we endured throughout our childhood. Maybe, if I would have stayed then things could have been different. For a while I talked myself into the idea that I was the cause of it all. I brainwashed myself into thinking I wasn't good enough. I suppose growing up the way I did will do that to a person.

After my beach encounter and when I finally began seeking answers, I sought out my mother because it was too difficult to swallow the idea I hadn't been worth the effort. I wanted to know *why* she didn't love us. With every sip of that bottle, every hit of the white powder, every needle in her vein, we became less important than her escape.

145

If forgiveness begins with an apology, would I be able to forgive her If she did apologize? I didn't think so. For years I contemplated whether or not she had ever been sorry for what she put us through. But not until my perspective changed, until I changed, did I learn that forgiveness was not about letting someone get away with what they had done, but instead, letting go of the power that person has over your mind, memories, and thoughts. Once you are able to let go of everything that haunts you and holds you down, you are able to learn and grow, and then, only then are you truly free.

For months, I was desperately trying to find myself again and I felt like she was the beginning to my ending. I got in touch with Lilian and she helped me track her down 40 miles out of town. Mother was alone in a trailer, living in the farmlands. There she lived a relatively content life, surrounded by wildlife. She enjoyed the wild hens that strutted through the flowers, feeding them occasionally. Sometimes if they let her, she would pet them. Those wild creatures brought her joy and she would linger in their presence for as long as possible before they fled into the yellow fields of flowers beyond the trailer. She always loved being right dab in the middle of nature. I guess we had that in common.

There in the wild, there was no pressure. Life had an entirely different meaning. Each moment in the tall fields of grass was a moment of beauty, of clarity. She was small compared to the world around her. *I bet she would have loved the beach.* There she would let the wind take her thoughts and rescue her worries, and with a little alcohol or prescription pills, there was nothing to worry about. Her life passed her by without trying.

She calmed down a lot in her later years but was still never going to be the mother I needed nor the friend I wanted. In my eyes, she was still as wild as those roaming hens and as free as the hawks that soared above her. She was an animal that refused to be tamed, and I understood that. So, I let her go but not before I had my answers. *Why was I never important enough? Why did you choose everyone and everything else but me? Didn't I matter?* As I stood there on the steps to her little white castle, grinding my teeth together, I felt a silent rage overtake me.

With a flurry of angry fists, I hit the trailer door, knocking so hard the trailer shook. *Answer the door Dana!* She always hated when I called her Dana, but mom wasn't fitting, so Dana it was. Banging on the door harder, I waited for her to answer. When she finally answered, and I saw her standing there on the creaky little staircase, my anger dissipated. The shaky metal door swung open, and suddenly the hairs on my arms stood up. Before me was someone that I didn't recognize. Her teeth were now missing, her hair wispy and withered. She looked like death and appeared much older than she really was. I felt sorry for her. She hadn't been paying attention as she opened the door, but when she recognized me, her eyes widened.

Removing the cigarette from her lips, she rolled the cherry between her fingers until it fell off and went out in the ashtray next to the door. As she stepped out into the light I could see her more clearly. The skin beneath her eyes sagged away from the sockets, and her eyes were bloodshot. Her hair was a tangled mess, and she wore clothes stained and wrinkled and much too large for her frail body. Though hesitant, I let her reel me in, and she began to cry. I couldn't believe it. I actually felt terrible for her. As those apologetic eyes swelling with tears bore down on me, I felt a great sadness wash over me, tearing at my seams. Stepping outside of my own shoes, it was in that moment that I realized how long it had genuinely been since she had seen her daughter. I was her first-born daughter, and I could tell she missed me, or at least the idea of what I could have been to her. I saw regret in those eyes, and I knew, without an exchange of words, that I could forgive her. Before she opened the door, I had fully intended to give her a piece of my mind, but suddenly everything changed.

The mere sound of her voice, the touch of her hand, and the teary-eyed smile touched me deeply. As quickly as the memories began to flood in, I started to flush them out, I had more control now. I knew it was time to let go of the hurt.

Forgiveness came to me like an unexpected storm in the middle of the night. I had held onto every memory, every sound, every ounce of the life I had before because I didn't know any other way. I didn't realize it until that day that holding onto all that pain only gave my abusers more power. I didn't want to give them that power anymore. I wanted to relinquish the pain I had endured because holding onto those memories and that hatred only kept me stagnant. I didn't want to be angry. I didn't want to cry myself to sleep. I didn't want to wake in the middle of the night, a sobbing mess for no reason. I wanted to be better, do better, and move on.

As I stood there in that doorway looking at the woman who gave birth to me, I forgave her. I let every inch of my body melt into that hug as she wrapped her arms around me and asked her how she had been.

I had always been different, and I hated that feeling. As a child, it took years before I was able to come to terms with the fact that I'd never be like anyone else. My mother would never hold my hand as we crossed the street. She would never tuck me in at night or give me cups of hot cocoa on cold winter days. I would probably never go on a family vacation. She'd never dress me for Prom, and I would probably never go to college. How could I even think about stupid things like prom and college when I could hardly stay in a house for more than a few months, let alone a school long enough to graduate. I never had the chance to experience things that most people took for granted.

I'll probably never know why she chose the path she did, even after her explanation. It will forever be a lingering question that I'll carry with me always.

My whole life I had longed for a nonexistent family that I hoped would one day come. I yearned for the things that were built-in for others. That natural bond that most children experience with their parents was stolen from me, swept out from beneath my feet by the very people who were supposed to love me most. I used to think I was broken, but now I see that I possess a delicate strength that has brought me to where I am today. My life experiences have changed me for the better. I'm not sure that I'll ever get over them or forget them, I've just learned how to be okay with them, and for now, that's okay with me.

As I stepped through the door to that tiny trailer, I noticed almost immediately that nothing about her had changed. She still painted, there were still empty bottles of booze lining the floors, and she still smelled of tobacco and liquor. Her words even moved with the same old slowness as she spoke, and I could tell she had been using again, "Oh, it's a new medication my doctor put me on" *Okay, Dana.* As I contemplated what to say next, she broke the silence with gifts. "Look, I got these for Lilah. I was hoping you could bring her over, and we could spend the night, have a slumber party? I'd like to see her." As she handed me a little set of mini nail polishes. "And look, I have this new eyeliner I thought you might like and look! Look here, I bet you would fit these shirts here," she stammered as she began pulling out articles of clothing from the wooden closet built into the trailer wall.

I let her take control of the conversation as I examined her, studied her, and silently judged her. The woman hadn't changed much, except for the fact that she was older now, and a bit slower with her words. I could tell she was excited to see me as she tried to appease me with a couple old t-shirts, so I indulged in her offerings. "Oh, that's cute! Thank you, I'll try them on later." I took a seat on the cushioned bench and began to think.

We sat there for hours talking, exchanging stories, and laughing at silly things that didn't matter. I shared a few stories with Dana and asked her a few about herself, hoping she would give me an explanation without me directly asking her. As we sat there talking, she began telling me of all the people that had hurt her in the same way they had hurt me. They took advantage of her, left her feeling broken.

She did the only thing she knew to feel better. I knew that she lacked strength and I knew that some people handle things terribly when faced with terrible circumstances. When I was a little girl, she was supposed to be my mother. She was supposed to take care of me, but she didn't. She couldn't, and I didn't know why until now. She was emotionally damaged, seeking solace in all the wrong ways.

I never saw her as a person before, never bothered to understand her until now. While listening to her babble on about her life, and her experience with drugs and drinking, I began to look at things differently. She was just a person with more children than she could handle, trying to get by in life while searching for someone to love her.

She made all the wrong choices, she did all the wrongs things, and I knew she was still making all the wrong decisions, but instead of hating her, I felt sorry for her. I no longer looked at her as my mother, or the woman who gave birth to me. She was just a person sitting next to me, rambling on about a lifetime of pain.

Drugs change you. The person you once were becomes obsolete. You lie, you steal, you cheat, and you stop caring about anyone and everyone you've ever loved. You're fixated on that next high, and without trying, you become addicted. Everything that was once important becomes less critical because now your only focus is how and when you can get more. It happens slowly, the spiral downward. Sometimes, you don't even recognize it until it's too late.

There was always a part of me that had hoped she would change. I thought watching her children leave would awaken something in her and she would become the person we needed again, but that never happened. I knew I needed to let go of this idea that she was going to be anything other than who she was, and after years of struggling, I'm finally okay with that. I still have bad days when I'm reminded of my childhood, because once you're a foster child, you're always a foster child. The only difference is that now, I'm not ashamed of who I am.

I left that trailer feeling differently than when I came in, I was still confused, but I was also proud of myself for tracking her down. Maybe everything that happened was for a reason. Perhaps all of these obstacles were only to prepare me for this new future I had ahead of me. The year of my 25th birthday had been one of the worst years of my life, but I definitely learned a few things.

As I walked down the dirt path and back to my car, I placed the gifts in my trunk and said goodbye, knowing that no matter what happened next, I could make it through. As I drove through the vineyards and sped toward home, I felt alive, like a weight was lifted off my soul. I promised myself that I would give Lilah everything I never had. If my parents taught me one thing, it was that I'll never be like either one of them. We all have a child within us that is fragile and just needs a little care. Sometimes I still feel like that little girl that needed someone to protect her, and that's okay. I'm unique, and it's those differences that make us beautiful.

I'm a different kind of dandelion, not a wilted flower like I was made to believe.

AUTHOR'S NOTE

Many of us come to a point in our lives when there is nothing that will numb the pain. Sometimes there isn't a drink or drug available that will fill the void in our hearts, so it's understandable that some children develop bad habits that are hard to break or fall into less-than-desirable situations out of the need to survive. It's a self-soothing mechanism that will only cause more turmoil. It's challenging to redirect those habits and pick up healthier, more functional habits or goals when you don't have a person to guide you. Believe it or not, there are former foster youth still struggling on their own as adults and just barely getting by.

In order to move on from my past, I needed to be ready and willing to be an emotional wreck in front of a total stranger, but it's difficult to sit down in front of someone you hardly know and bare your soul openly. Once I was able to come to terms with the fact that I was still battling with emotional trauma as an adult, it was definitely the most beneficial thing I could have done for my mental health, and I encourage anyone going through a difficult time to seek help. Sometimes talking to a complete stranger is all you need.

I hope that my book will help anyone who is currently going through, or has struggled and dealt with, situations similar to mine, I know that children in foster care have experienced a life that most people couldn't possibly imagine. Each story is unique and traumatic in its own way, and when life slows down and the haze clears, all we are left with are fragments of memories and moments in time that have altered our existence. **It's how we choose to live with those memories that will define our future.**

To everyone who has ever been exposed to the foster care system, may my words guide you through the darkest of times and become a beacon of hope through shared experiences. Remember that no matter what you've been lead to believe your whole life, you are worthy. You can make a difference. You do matter, and you can achieve your goals as long as you have the motivation to fight and fight hard. Your past has made you a survivor. There will be times when you won't believe it, but I promise you it's true. You are a stronger person because of what you've been through, and you will learn to use that strength, that power, to inspire change in others and in yourself as you wildly chase your dreams. Anything is possible as long as you believe in yourself. Don't be afraid to dream and dream big.

These life experiences that I've had to deal with changed me, and it took years before I was able to cope with those changes. I spent so many years feeling as though life had cheated me of everything. In fact, I'm in my mid-twenties now, and I'm still trying to figure life out, especially when it comes to forming friendships and developing bonds. Throughout my childhood, I never let anyone close and rebelled consistently.

Today, I'm very selective about the few people that I keep close because the truth is, I'm just not good at keeping friends. I'm still learning how to love people, how to "let people in." I'm great at making friends but keeping them is a different story. Trust me, it's not because I like being alone or don't want to have people in my life, but over time I've learned that people will inevitably let you down in one way or another, and I prefer to avoid uncomfortable situations. At least that's what I was conditioned to learn at an early age - that people will fail you.

It wasn't until I was able to overcome many adverse situations with the help of other people did I realized everything I had learned to believe was wrong. It took a while before I could trust the idea that people weren't "out to get me" or going to hurt me, because as a child I was conditioned to believe otherwise. You can either succumb to your life experiences and let them control you, or you can learn from them, growing into a bigger, better, and stronger person. It's not easy, and truth be told, I lost myself momentarily.

For a while I didn't think I would be able to bounce back after everything I had been through, and for a while I gave up on trying. When it finally happened, it wasn't quick, it wasn't a "bounce." It took a long time. I had to truly understand and learn the deeper meaning behind the things that haunted me. I had to undergo a few otherworldly experiences before I was able to see a brighter future. A future where my story, and everything I went through, mean something. It's only now, ten years after leaving my old life behind, that I can finally say *"I'm okay."* Well, at least I try and be okay. Sometimes all we can do is try, and that's *okay* with me.

AKNOLEDGEMENTS

To every person I've ever encountered throughout the years, thank you for everything you've taught me. Whether good or bad, it's made me who I am today.

To my girls, my husband, Brenna, Laura, Juan, James, Camelia, Elijah, Jacob, Jonathan, Alexis, Brandyn, Patrick, Gabby, Venessa, Chad, Teresa, Gerry, Debbie, Steve, Erik, Matt, Mike, Denise, Desaree, Paula, Sandra, Kathy, Stephanie, Brieanna, Nandie, Larry, Stephen, Rob, Norma, Janisha, Kat, Teresa, Mary, Lucy, David, Henry, Jason, Shannon, Kimberly, Daniel, Jessica, Katelyn, Erin, Julie and Sally, I'm so glad to know or have known you. Thank you for all of your help, support, guidance, and for being a big part of my life when I needed you the most. I love you.

When ▮▮▮ and I were little you took care of us you put us before yourself and you'd kick anyones ass if they were to dare call us a name HAHA but ▮▮▮ as we grew older life became harder and I dont know how you took care of us. mom was always gone but you were always there. I dont know how you did it being so young teenager. You had the worst of it at of all of us. you went through hell. your the strongest person I know. you taught me well. and you still began to teach me! ▮▮▮ Thankyou for everything you did for me and ▮▮▮ in our lives. I know if you werent there, It would have been so much worse for us thankyou ▮▮▮ I love you♡

-Lillian, written at 18 years old

life gets hard, but
one thing you taught me is
that if you're happy well then
its okay, I would have
never been who I am if
it wasn't for you I look
up to you now and when
I was a child. You were
my first best friend and idol,
yeah we had some good memories
when we were little, like when
we were chased by a big dog
walking home from school when
we lived on ███████████

When we were split
up, It was so hard I cried
so much. I was lost without
you I became the oldest, I
had know clue what to do,
Dad was a stranger everything
became a stranger even the people
I knew. But I always thought
of you, It help... alot!
lifes hard things
happen we learn. We become
who we are because of that

-Lillian, written at 18 years old

Hi, I am writing to you in candle light because I still don't feel like turning on the light but you'll be happy to know I'm no longer hiding in my closet, my ~~dark~~ dark and comfy closet. I don't know what to write you but I guess I'll write whatever comes to my head.

You nailed it when we were talking. You said I was happy but sad, well I am. I am so very depressed when I am not doing anything or when I am alone that I want to die right there, but I remember you as a friend.

You have been such a ~~good great~~ great friend that all I really miss is the times we've had together. The same goes with ████████ At night when I sleep, during showers, church, school/homework, really unless something requires my full attention I am thinking about you two. My two bestest friends in the world and everything we did together.

I guess those days are officially over but I still have my dreams Oh, boy that sounds corny but its ~~true~~ true. Man I keep miss spelling simple (ra) words, Sorry. And my ~~and writing~~ writing is very sloppy.

-Piper, written at 15 years old

You Are My
Best Friend
But I have
to Go. I'll
write you again
Soon

P.s. Don't forget
The Old Me

See you wendsday
because nothing is
going to stop me from
ice skating.

-Piper, written at 15 years old

My Life   To: mom
           only
Its a reck there is 1 person I hate
We all hate 1 person I don't like
you know who that person is. Time is
a thing I go call useable my time is
▓ vallubnt time. So I'm good at plans.
▓▓▓▓ is like me he hates that ... 1 person
family is only by blood I call 19 and 37's
bad she knows that well thats none of
my buissness if thing Doen't get straitn
up... bye... bye... See now you
get it Don't you I know thing
arent always going my way but I can't stand
having a mother not beliving me and I have
none so mad you won't understand so for
▓▓▓▓ I love you for ▓▓▓▓ love you
to for mom love you only when you
love me and you belive me. You have never herd
what ▓▓▓▓▓▓▓ me was are you
going to belive me?

-Parker, written at 8 years old

Dear Mom
I love you and miss you.
how is every body doing down
there. we are doing fine. Are
you still whith ▓▓▓▓ How come
it took you a month to write us?
I hope you are fine. Are the
animals doing fine. We are
sad and we miss you. We get
in trouble a lot for doing some things
a tiny little wrong. Write back
soon.

-Lillian, written at 11 years old

D Unit Rules

1) Be sure you are properly dressed when you exit your room; shirts tucked in, pants cuffed and pulled up to your waist- do not expose your shorts or underwear.
2) Wristbands are to be worn at all times. Do not alter or destroy your wristband- this will result in Room Confinement.
3) Graffiti is not allowed on the walls, desks, beds, sinks, etc.
4) Boy/girl interaction is not allowed.
5) Do not keep food in your room or dorm. Food is to be eaten during meals or rec program and discarded.
6) Food trading/giving away is not allowed.
7) Garbage is not to be thrown on the dorm floors until evening unit cleanup.
8) Do not talk in the hallway.
9) Do not look in windows, even your own.
10) Do not look out of your window or dorm window
11) No gang agitation.
12) Do not drink water from the water fountain without permission.
13) Do not ask to be a worker.
14) Do not ask for food. (Workers, food is a privilege, not a right.)
15) No talking during controlled television.
16) Open rec. talking is allowed at minimum. No talking between tables.
17) Don't get out of your seat without permission.
18) Males have a total of 8 minutes for shower and hygiene, while females have a total of 10 minutes.
19) No lotion or grease is allowed in your dorm or room. Grease is given during morning hygiene only, while lotion is only given after evening showers.
20) You may braid hair with staff permission during courtyard free-time or during a movie, if staff allow. No opposite sex braiders.
21) Residents in the dorms must face the wall while sleeping and keep their feet off the floor when sitting on their beds. Residents in the small dorm may be asked to turn around and face the cabinets during controlled television. Residents in the large dorm are not allowed to sit at or on their desks.
22) No phones before 3 p.m. on school days or if you are a level one.
23) Boys are not allowed to have rubber bands.

*All rules are subject to change for any reason, anytime, by any staff!

Caseload Worker: ▓▓▓▓▓▓▓▓

-D Unit Rules

From: ▓▓▓▓▓▓▓▓▓▓n.edu]
Sent: ▓▓▓▓▓▓▓▓▓2007 11:20 AM
To: ▓▓▓▓▓▓▓
Subject: re: ▓▓▓▓▓▓

▓▓▓▓▓appears happy and well adjusted this year, especially when compared to last school year. In serving as her school counselor, I have worked on a regular basis with ▓▓▓▓ having observed her in our school play where she displayed outstanding talent, her attendance is improving steadily this year, and I don't believe that her most recent grades are indicative of what she can actually do. I would assume that there will be future grade improvement.

Any interactions that I have experienced with her foster mother have been positive and it is apparent that her current living situation is working to ▓▓▓▓ advantage. It would be a disruption and a disadvantage to take away the consistency and emotional stability that ▓▓▓▓ has been experiencing in her foster care placement this school year.

Sincerely,
▓▓▓▓▓▓▓▓▓s Counselor

-High School Counselor, 2007

Dear To Whom It May Concern,

With great pleasure I recommend ▓▓▓▓▓▓▓ as a dynamic, excellent, and dedicated student. ▓▓▓▓ has been a student in the AVID program at ▓▓▓▓▓▓▓▓▓ School. In her classes, ▓▓▓▓ exhibited strong written and verbal communication skills, and a determination to succeed academically.

Along with her academic skills, ▓▓▓▓ possesses exceptional leadership and influence by having a positive attitude and sense of determination. There once was a time when ▓▓▓▓ grade point average was 1.0, but just last term she received a 3.25 grade point average. She has overcome many obstacles, academically and socially, proving that she is goal oriented and willing to go above and beyond to be successful. Having a positive attitude, ▓▓▓ greets me with a smile daily, and is always willing to help others in class. Viewing difficulties as challenges, she has proven that she will not rest from any task until she produces the very best results.

Without hesitation, I recommend ▓▓▓▓▓▓ for either your school's AVID program or any program that enables her to remain on track for college.

Please contact me if you have any questions.

Best regards,
▓▓▓▓▓▓▓▓▓▓▓▓▓
AVID Coordinator
▓▓▓▓Teacher

-HS AVID Coordinator,